HISTORY, MYSTERY, *and* HAUNTINGS *of* SOUTHERN ILLINOIS

I hope you enjoy all
history, mystery and
hauntings that
Southern Illinois
has to offer.

[signature]

Thank You Hope you
enjoy our book!
Happy Hauntings!
[signature]

HISTORY, MYSTERY, *and* HAUNTINGS *of* SOUTHERN ILLINOIS

By

BRUCE L. CLINE AND LISA A. CLINE

History, Mystery, and Hauntings of Southern Illinois

First Printing Summer 2011

ISBN-10: 0-9790401-1-6
ISBN-13: 978-0-9790401-1-5

To order copies of this book contact:

Black Oak Media
Rockford, Illinois
www.blackoakmedia.org
orders@blackoakmedia.org

Printed in the United States of America.

This book is dedicated to our ghost detecting cats - Fluffy, Flopsie, Mittens, Highway and our ghost detecting dogs – Palin and Caeser.

Acknowledgments

Bruce Cline would like to thank the Little Egypt Ghost Society team of professionals who helped make this book possible. His wife, Lisa – Co-founder and investigator, Kale Meggs – Investigator and historical researcher, Susan Hafford Brown – Investigator, Joe Rieckenberg – investigator, Rich McLevich – Reiki Master, Suzanne Gorrell – Researcher.

Special thanks to Sandy Vinyard – Manager of the Rose Hotel, Scott Thorne – Ghost historian and owner of Castle Perilous Games, Michael Kleen – Founder and publisher of Black Oak Media, and Matt Hucke – Graveyard explorer. Your advice, stories and encouragement meant a lot to me.

I would also like to thank the following for proofreading the manuscript. Emily Morton, Daniell Weinhoffer and Kristin Horstmann.

Table of Contents

Forward

As the earliest part of the state to be settled by Europeans, southern Illinois is steeped in history. From the French settlements at Cahokia, Fort de Chartres, Fort Massac, and Kaskaskia, to the convulsions of the American Civil War, to the present day, the region popularly known as "Little Egypt" has been filled with legends, folklore, and ghost stories. For those interested in ghost lore, southern Illinois offers some of the oldest ghost stories in the state.

And why should it not? Anywhere a majestic lodge like the Rose Hotel can stand for nearly two centuries is bound to be haunted by some specters of the past. These strange tales go all the way back to 1719 when the French brought slaves from Santo Domingo to the Mississippi River. Some of these slaves, they feared, possessed supernatural powers, and at least one paid for it with his life.

As far as the folklore of southern Illinois is concerned, two books stand out: *Legends & Lore of Southern Illinois* by John W. Allen and *Tales and Songs of Southern Illinois* by Charles Neely. One was published in the 1930s and the other in the 1960s. Not much has been written on the subject since then, and so when Bruce approached me about publishing his book on the legends and lore of southern Illinois, I was very excited.

Some of the stories in this book are old favorites, but many are brand new. Bruce has not only read about these places, in many cases he has been there partaking in the story itself. That is a rare quality. I have no doubt that readers will find many surprises contained within the pages of this book.

Michael Kleen
Rock River Valley
Summer 2011

LITTLE EGYPT

COUNTIES

LITTLE EGYPT

COUNTY SEATS

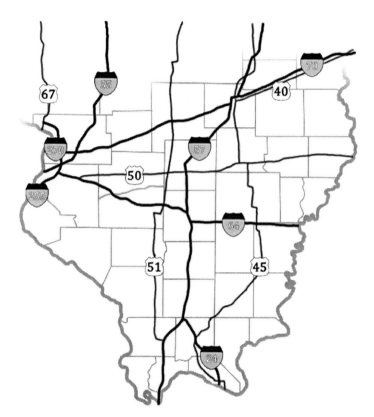

LITTLE EGYPT
MAJOR HIGHWAYS

Bruce L. Cline and Lisa A. Cline

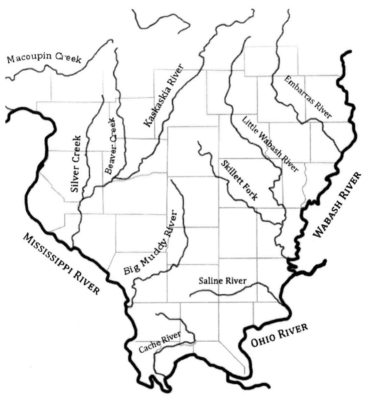

LITTLE EGYPT

PRINCIPAL WATERWAYS

14

Introduction

My interest in ghosts and the paranormal started at an early age. When I was about eight or nine years old, I had my first ghostly encounter. My brother and I were spending the night at our grandparent's house in Marion, Illinois. After a fun day of play in the garden and woodshed, we retired for the night. Of the three bedrooms in the house, we were to sleep in the middle bedroom. At some point during the night, I woke up and noticed a dark shadow on the wall opposite the window. It was a shadow of a large dog or wolf-like creature. There were no pets in the house to make such a shadow. I was so scared that I pulled the covers over my head and did not sleep the rest of the night.

A couple of years later in 1966, a new TV show came out that was called "*Dark Shadows.*" The show was about a 175 year old vampire named Barnabas Collins. I rushed home from school every day to watch it. I was fascinated with the idea of vampires and the paranormal. Instead of fear, I became curious and started studying all things paranormal as well as folklore and history. This led me to start a club that I called the "Gaslight Ghoul Club." Members of this club would spend many late night hours around campfires or in my tree house telling spooky stories.

Eventually, college, careers and raising a family took up much of my time. It wasn't until 2007 that my wife Lisa and I started the Little Egypt Ghost Society. We were interested in ghost hunting, but we were also interested in history and mysteries. The way we approach the paranormal is to research the history behind the stories. Once you know the history of a person, location or thing, there may be some mystery associated with the historical events. We found that many times, there is a haunting associated with the mysteries that history has to offer.

Once we became established as credible paranormal investigators and historians, we started receiving many calls from individuals and businesses seeking our help with what they considered paranormal activity. Our group is made up of skeptics, optimistic skeptics to be exact. We use research as well as "ghost hunting" equipment to document and try to arrive at a logical explanation for reported paranormal activity. Only after we have ruled out all naturally occurring and logical explanations do we consider that the events may have a paranormal explanation.

The stories that you will read in this book, come from our case files, local history and folklore. Like most people, the members of the Little Egypt Ghost Society enjoy a good spooky story. While we won't vouch for the truth of every story presented, we will state that they all have been told to us as being the truth. We hope that you enjoy the stories presented in this book as well as the history, mystery and hauntings that are to be found in southern Illinois.

Bruce L. Cline, Director
LITTLE EGYPT GHOST SOCIETY
Carbondale, Illinois
Spring 2011

Why we are called "The Little Egypt Ghost Society"

Southern Illinois is known as "Little Egypt" due to a strange coincidence between the southern tip of Illinois and ancient Egypt. If you turn to the Bible you will find a story about a great famine. The patriarch Jacob upon hearing there was corn in Egypt; said to his sons, "Why, look ye on one another. Behold, I have heard there is corn in Egypt; go you down there, etc." Further reading from the Bible will reveal that when the famine was over all the earth the storehouses or granaries of Egypt were opened and all the other countries came to Egypt to buy corn.

The wickedly cold winter of 1830-1831, known as the "Deep Snow," was the longest and most severe ever recorded in Illinois. These frigid conditions resulted in little or no corn being planted in the state of Illinois in 1831 north of Jefferson County until the month of June. To add to this disaster, there was a heavy, killing frost on the night of September 10, 1831, which destroyed many of the late crops in Illinois. In fact, all corn crops north of the 38th latitude were completely ruined.

1832 was known as the great "Corn Famine" in Illinois. The entire state north of the 38th latitude had no corn and had to bring it in from other locations. The counties in the southern tip of Illinois starting at Jefferson County and the ones adjoining it all had plenty of corn. The farmers of southern Illinois began shipping their corn to the counties to the north. The people of the time, remembering the Biblical story of the 10 sons of Jacob going down to Egypt for corn, began telling others that they "have heard there is corn in Egypt, and have come to

17

buy for ourselves." This is the origin of southern Illinois being called "Little Egypt." Today, all of southern Illinois is very proud of its heritage and the endearing nickname of Little Egypt.

When we formed our ghost hunting and paranormal investigation team in 2007, we wanted a name that would reflect the history, mystery and hauntings of southern Illinois. After much research and thought, we chose to call ourselves the Little Egypt Ghost Society.

What in the Devil?

It seems that the Devil has staked a claim in southern Illinois. Many sites and areas in Little Egypt are named in honor of the diabolical one.

Grand Tower is the home of several landmarks named for the Prince of Darkness. Along the Mississippi River are rocky hills known as the Devil's Backbone. Just to the north is a hill known as the Devil's Bake Oven where iron was produced in brick lined ovens, the remains of which can still be seen today. On the far side of the river is an island known as Tower Rock and just downstream is an area known as the Devil's Whirlpool. Many boats and lives have been lost here.

- In Giant City State Park there is a rock formation that resembles a table that is known as the Devil's Stand Table.
- A few miles east of Giant City State Park is Devil's Kitchen Lake. The lake was created when a rock creek bed had a dam built across it. The creek bed contained a deep pool that was known as Devil's Well.
- Bell Smith Springs is the home of a natural stone bridge known as Satan's Backbone.
- A few miles south of Steeleville one can find Rock Castle Creek. The creek has two deep holes known as Little Devil's Hole and Big Devil's Hole.

- There is a valley in Union County known as You Be Damned Hollow. Hell's Half Acre can be found in Lawrence County.

If you speak of the Devil and want to go to Hell and back, you need look no further than Little Egypt.

Named by Death

Death leaves its mark wherever it goes. Several southern Illinois towns and landmarks received their names from some connection with death, or death is all that remains of them.

- In 1839, Bainbridge was the first seat of Williamson County. Today, Bainbridge exists as a very small cemetery on Bainbridge Trail Road and is now part of Marion.
- Dog Hollow is a valley in Pope County. It is located 12 miles south of Harrisburg. A local legend told by John W. Allen is that "Two young men had seen their girls safely home from a church service. They were returning at a late hour through the hollow. By their story they were pursued by a headless dog. Thus the hollow received its name and has ever since been called Dog Hollow."
- Ellis Mound in Hamilton County received its name from the Ellis family who buried one of their children near the trail as they passed through the area in the 1880s.

- Lively Grove in Washington County received its name when the John Lively family was killed by Indians in 1813.

- Rector Township in Saline County received its name from John Rector who was killed by Shawnee Indians near Rector Creek in 1805.

- Rosiclare in Hardin County received its name from the daughters of an early settler who were drowned in a boating accident. Their names were Rose and Clare.

- Schoharie Prairie in Williamson County received its name when a band of vigilantes were whipping a hog thief. One of the vigilantes yelled out, "Score him, Harry!" The site has been known as Scoreharry and then Schoharrie ever since.

- Vancil Bend, a loop in the Big Muddy River in Williamson County received its name after Isaac Vancil, an early settler, was hanged by vigilantes when he refused to leave the area.

- Wartrace in Johnson County received its name when a veteran returned home from the Civil War and stole a horse after killing the owner. The man was captured, given a quick trial, and then hanged. Citizens of the community decided to rename it Wartrace hoping that the incident would be the last trace of the Civil War.

Alexander County

Cairo Masonic Lodge

Many paranormal occurrences have been reported in the Cairo Masonic Lodge # 237, AF&AM. Lodge members say that the building is haunted by one of its Past Masters by the name of Harry August Eichoff. Harry was born on February 15, 1864 and died in Cairo, Illinois on May 30, 1937. His funeral service was conducted on the second floor of the Masonic Lodge.

Most of the paranormal activity occurs on the second and third floors. Some of the strange things reported are the sounds of heavy footsteps, cold spots, the feeling that someone is watching you from behind, doors that were shut only to be found open later. Three lights next to the altar will turn on after being turned off, locker doors that will open without explanation and cameras that fail to take photos.

The Little Egypt Ghost Society was invited by members of the Cairo Masonic Lodge #237, AF&AM to conduct a paranormal investigation of the lodge. Shortly after our investigations team arrived at the lodge to interview some of the lodge members, we discovered that the new batteries that we had just put in one of our digital cameras and two of the digital voice recorders were dead!

After interviewing the members, we were taken on a tour of the lodge. We all took numerous, interesting photos. After leaving each area, I reviewed my digital photos to make sure they turned out OK. Upon going to a new area of the lodge, I discovered that my previous photos were missing! I returned to re-photograph the area, and much to my dismay... the photos were mysteriously erased again! I took some more photos and reviewed them to make sure they were all there. When we finally left the lodge, we all met in the parking lot to discuss what we had found. When I checked my digital cameras to show off the great shots I captured, I discovered that all of my photos had been erased again!

It seemed like the spirits at the Masonic Lodge did not want us to leave with any photos on our cameras. 'My theory is that since I am a Master Mason and swore a "blood oath" not to reveal secrets of the Masonic Lodge, the spirit of Harry would not let me break my oath by revealing any "secrets" with my camera.

Effingham County

Colonel Greathouse

During a visit to the Old City Cemetery in Vandalia, I decided to use my PX ITC experimental device. I was getting no results until I was at the grave of Colonel Lucien Philip Greathouse. As soon as I stepped foot on his grave, the PX device said "MARTYR and COUNTRY."

Colonel Greathouse commanded Company C of the 48th Illinois Infantry. At the battle of Peach Tree Creek on July 22, 1864, rebels used a large brick house owned by Troupe Hurtt as a stronghold. At this time, Lucien, now a Colonel and commander of the 48th, was ordered to seize the house and destroy the rebel occupants. Riding a large claybank horse, and with saber in hand, Col. Greathouse led the charge. With the rebels in pursuit of the broken Union line, one of them yelled, "Surrender, can't you see you are beaten?"

Col. Greathouse replied, "Beat hell, we've just come into the fight!" At that moment a Minié ball struck him in the chest and he was immediately killed. His age at the time of his death was 22 years, 1 month and 15 days.

The body of Colonel Greathouse was returned to Vandalia and buried in Old City Cemetery. A 16 foot granite monument was placed on his grave detailing the battle in which he had participated. It also contained the following inscription:

His Example was Worth a Thousand Men,
Gen. W. T. Sherman. The Bravest man in the Army

of the Tennessee, Gen. J. A. Logan. He led the command in forty hard fought battles and was killed with the flag of his regiment and country in his hands standing upon the breast works of the enemy before the city of Atlanta, GA in the memorable fight of July 22, 1864. May his God and his Country deal justly by him. LUCIEN GREATHOUSE, COLONEL U. S. ARMY. BORN CARLNSVILLE, ILINOIS 7TH DAY OF JUNE 1842 A.D. AND WAS KILLED AT THE HEAD OF HIS REGIMENT BEFORE ATLANTA, GEORGIA 22ND JULY 1864 A.D. WE CANNOT WIN HIM BACK.

Recently, a marble stone containing the same inscriptions was placed at the foot of the grave. This new marble stone contains a mystery. Colonel Greathouse was in the U.S. Army at the time of his death, why then, is the stone engraved with the insignia of a U.S. Naval officer and 2 stars of a general?

Franklin County

The Water Witch and Ghost of Mr. Joab at The Diggins

Franklin County was extremely dry one summer in the 'mid-1800s. It was so dry that the residents of Barren Township decided to bring in a water witch to find water for the thirsty community. Every place that was indicated as having water only produced dry wells. After many attempts at finding water with negative results, the water witch said, "Well, we will just have to call this place 'The Diggins'!"

From that point on, this small section in the southeast corner of Barren Township was known as "The Diggins." This area is located east of the Rend Lake Conservation Office and water treatment plant.

There used to be a log cabin on Joab's Hill on the east side of "The Diggins" that was haunted by the ghost of Mr. Joab. Many of the older folk around the area would tell their kids late night stories about it.

Gallatin County

The Old Slave House

John Hart Crenshaw built this three story southern plantation style mansion on top Hickory Hill near Equality in the 1830s. Crenshaw rented salt wells from the State of Illinois and began making salt. This business venture made him a rich man. The work at the salt wells was performed mainly by slaves from Kentucky and Tennessee. The Illinois Constitution of 1818, Article VI, Section 2 reads: "No person bound to labor in any other State shall be hired to labor in this State, except within the tract reserved for the salt works near Shawneetown; nor even at that place for a longer period than one year at a time, nor shall it be allowed there after the year 1825. Any violation of this article shall effect the emancipation of such person from obligation to service."

This legal loophole enabled John Hart Crenshaw to become even wealthier. Crenshaw would lease slaves from Livingston County, Kentucky across the river from Shawneetown for $150 a year. Being a shrewd businessman, Crenshaw was always on the lookout for new ways to increase his profits. His solution was to create a "reverse underground railroad." Slaves who escaped to the "Free" State of Illinois were captured by Crenshaw and put to work at the salt wells. Some of these slaves were sold back to plantation owners in Kentucky and then leased from the new owners to work in the salt wells. Although the slave-napping business was a very good source of labor and income for Crenshaw, it was still not enough. There was a special breeding room on the third floor where a huge black slave named "Uncle Bob" would be bred with selected females in order to produce a stronger breed or strain of worker that would be of exceptional strength for the salt wells.

To prevent prying eyes from spying on his new business venture, Crenshaw had a secret passageway built into his house so that the wagons containing the kidnapped slaves could be driven inside the mansion and unloaded at night. They were then taken to the third floor slave quarters of the mansion. The third floor contained several narrow cells that measured 6 feet by 2 feet. There was an area that contained a whipping post, shackles, and heavy balls and chains.

On one occasion when Crenshaw was whipping some "uppity" females, several other slaves attacked him with an ax, severing his leg. This understandably angered Crenshaw even more and resulted in even harsher treatment of the slaves.

Today, John Hart Crenshaw and his slaves are long gone. What remains, however, are the stories of cruel and inhuman treatment, and of ghosts. The third floor of his manor in particular is known for many stories of hauntings. There have been reports of shrieks, groans, and the sound of slaves crying in the night. Other sounds manifested were that of chains rattling and whips cracking over the naked backs of the slaves. Misty forms would be seen just out of the corner of one's eyes. The third floor quarters have a very malevolent and sad feeling to them. Many years ago, visitors were allowed to spend the night in the third floor slave quarters to experience the ghostly activity for themselves. In the 1920s, an exorcist came to spend the night with the intent of ridding the mansion of its ghosts. During the night, the exorcist came running out of mansion and collapsed on the lawn. He had died of fright. In the 1960's, two Marines (both Vietnam War veterans) tried to spend the night in the third floor quarters, but fled in terror.

Today, the Old Slave House is owned by the State of Illinois. It is closed to the public.

The Old Slave House Stud

"Uncle Bob" Wilson was one of the slaves known to have lived at the Hickory Hill Plantation, now known as the Old Slave House outside Equality, Illinois. Crenshaw was infamous for his "Reverse Underground Railroad." He would kidnap free negroes and sell them across the river in Kentucky as slaves.

The supply of kidnapped slaves was not enough to supply slave trade, so Crenshaw used the services of "Uncle Bob" as a stud on his plantation. Whenever Crenshaw had young female slaves, he would have them chained to Uncle Bob's bed for breeding purposes. This "slave factory" produced hundreds of children to be sold as slaves.

During the Civil War, Uncle Bob Wilson joined the Confederate Army and proudly served with the 16th Virginia Infantry as an orderly to a Confederate Officer.

After the war, he became a Baptist minister. In the 1920s he moved back to Gallatin County. Then, sometime after the 1937 flood that nearly destroyed Shawneetown, he moved to Chicago. In 1942 he was moved to the Elgin State Hospital and was the oldest resident at the veteran's home there. Uncle Bob Wilson lived to be 112 years old and said that the secret to his long life was, "I never drank, chewed or stayed out late until I was 11 years old."

The Old Salt Works

For over 200 years this ancient salt spring has been the location of much tragedy and violence. It is located in Gallatin County north of Illinois Route 1 and west of the Old Slave House. The Old Spring and Salt Works are difficult to find from the lonely gravel road that passes by it. If you look closely enough you might be able to catch a glimpse of the timbers that frame the hole in the ground that forms the Old Well.

Once you find the well, you will immediately be overcome with sulfur like, rotten egg stench and the smell of decaying vegetation. Once you venture off the gravel road and into the blue mud of the creek bed, you will be immediately attacked by thousands of hungry mosquitoes.

There is a very eerie and haunting feeling that will envelope you as you peer into the bluish, bubbling waters of the salt well. Many people have reported feeling like they were being watched by unseen eyes from the surrounding forest. 'It is like you are being watched by the spirits of the ancient Indians, slaves and maybe even the mastodons, buffalo and murdered souls who once paused at the very spot that you are standing on.

Never go to this place alone!

Hardin County

The Rose Hotel in Elizabethtown

This is the most haunted place the Little Egypt Ghost Society has ever investigated, and we consider the Rose Hotel to be one of the most haunted places in America. We have conducted several overnight searches for the spirits still lingering at this historic and famous hotel.

In 1813, James McFarlan received a license to operate a tavern in Elizabethtown. The McFarlan family charged 25 cents for breakfast, dinner or supper, lodging for 12 ½ cents, a gallon of oats or corn cost 12 ½ cents, a half pint of whiskey went for $1.25, a quart of beer was

12 ½ cents. The tavern was famous for drinks such as taffia, cherry bounce and cider royal.

The McFarlan family operated the tavern until 1890 when it was purchased by Mrs. Sarah Rose. At that time the name was changed to the Rose Hotel. Mrs. Rose operated the hotel for 55 years with the help of Frankie and Tote Woods.

The oldest wing of the hotel was built about 1830, with additions built about 1848 and 1866. Today, the exterior is restored to its 1866 appearance. In 1972, the Rose Hotel was added to the National Register of Historic Places. The Rose hotel is now owned by the Historic Sites Division of the Illinois Historic Preservation Agency and is operated by Sandy Vinyard as a bed and breakfast.

Sandy Vinyard invited the Little Egypt Ghost Society to investigate reports of the paranormal activity that has been occurring at the hotel on a regular basis. Sandy and many of her guests have reported sounds coming from parts of the hotel (it only has six guest rooms) where no one is present. These noises are said to sound like there "is a party going on up there." Objects have been mysteriously moved, only to reappear sometime later in a different location of the hotel. Pennies, in groups of three, are found on a continuous basis throughout the hotel.

Our team captured the image of one of the former servants, Tote Wilson, in a mirror in the McFarlan Suite. The image was positively identified by Sandy Vinyard using the hotel scrap book containing old photographs of the hotel and staff. We tried to debunk our photo, even going so far as to video tape the entire process, but could not reproduce the image.

We conducted several EVP experiments while at the hotel with very interesting results:

Q. "Are you alone?" A. "YES"

Q. "How do you feel?' A. "FINE"

Q. "Where are y you now?" A. "RIGHT BEHIND YOU"

Another EVP captured with our camcorder said: "WE ARE YOUR BEST FRIENDS"

We set up motion detectors throughout the hotel. At approximately 3:00 AM, the motion detector in the Charlotte Room went off repeatedly with corresponding EMF reading of 2.3 to 2.6 milligauss.

In the front lobby we took a photograph about midnight that showed the face of a young lady looking in the front window. There was no one outside at the time. This photograph was positively identified by Sandy Vinyard as one of her former workers who was killed in a car crash about a year earlier.

On several occasions, our group would smell the scent of cigars, bacon cooking, lavender and logs burning when none of those items were present in or near the hotel. We heard voices and the sound of a small dog barking as well as footsteps and doors creaking open and shuts upstairs when no one was up there.

There is a small graveyard behind the hotel where several members of the McFarlan family as well as some of the servants and guests are buried. Many of the graves are unmarked.

On October 5, 2009, I was standing in the center of the McFarlan Suite in total darkness and took this photo with my digital camera and flash. I was the only living person in the room at the time. Note the image of a man looking out of the far left corner of the mirror. We went back to this room Feb 11, 2010 and tried to debunk this photo. No matter what we did, we could not recapture Tote's image in the mirror. This photo is positively paranormal.

Sandy Vineyard positively identified the man as "Tote" from a photograph in the hotel scrapbook. Tote was a servant at the hotel many years ago.

This is a close up view of Tote's ghost in mirror in the McFarlan Suite of the Rose Hotel.

The night before this photo was taken; I was conducting an Electronic Voice Phenomena (EVP) experiment. One of the questions I asked was "will you join us for breakfast in the morning." We believe these orbs could be the spirits of Frankie, Tote and Mammy Rose.

In early spring of 2010, the Little Egypt Ghost Society was at the Rose Hotel to film a TV commercial.

After filming, we decided to do a little ghost hunting in the McFarlan Suite. Sandy Vinyard was present with us when she heard the floor start to "creak." At that moment, Lisa and I started getting readings on our K2 and Ghost Meter EMF meters. We were able to trace the EMF field to a location near the center of the suite. We quickly realized that the EMF field was confined to an area the size and shape of an adult human! When we placed our hands into this EMF field, we discovered that the temperature was 15 to 20 degrees cooler than the surrounding area. At that point, the EMF field moved and we tracked it to an area near the fire place. Once again, the temperature inside the EMF field was noticeably cooler than the surrounding area. At this point the electric power went off in the McFarlan Suite, but not in any other area of the hotel. After we exited the suite, the power mysteriously came back on. We then rechecked the entire suite and could not relocate the EMF field. We firmly believe that this was the spirit of Tote Wood once again playfully letting us know that he still keeps watch over the nearly 200 year old Rose Hotel.

Ahab Gullett

Legend has it that, if you go to the small creek at the far end of Pleasant Hill Cemetery near Karber's Ridge in Hardin County at night, you will hear bells ringing and the sound of a gate opening and closing. There is a spirit there that allegedly haunts the cemetery. The name of the spirit is Ahab Gullet. His tombstone, located near the entrance of the cemetery, reads: "Friends beware as you pass by, as you are now so once was I. As I am you soon shall be, prepare for death and follow me." If you read this aloud, it is said that spirits will appear before you. My group of paranormal investigators decided to investigate this site one tranquil fall evening.

We started at Ahab Gulletts' gravestone and read the inscription aloud. We then headed to the back side of the cemetery to the creek. As we approached the edge of the creek, the wind began to pick up and the trees began to sway. The water was very shallow and crystal clear with a solid rock bottom. As I stepped to the edge of the water a horseshoe appeared right in front of my eyes along the bottom. I reached down into the water and retrieved it. Seconds later, another horseshoe was found by another investigator. We had a total of five investigators present that night. How many horseshoes did we find? Five. These horseshoes have been estimated to be over 100 years old.

The Ghost of Dr. Anna Bigsby

Hardin County is infamous for river pirates, highwaymen, murderers and various other miscreants.

However, Hardin County is also known for kind hearted, hardworking and respected people as well. Anna Bigsby was one of the latter.

When Anna was 16 about years old, she came to southern Illinois from Philadelphia in a covered wagon with her parents. Anna was well educated and became a teacher. She was strong, fearless and able to take care of herself. According to legend, Anna once killed a man who attempted to attack her. Soon afterward, she returned to Philadelphia to study medicine. Upon completion of medical school, Anna returned to southern Illinois as a doctor, teacher and church worker. She married a farmer's son named Isaac Hobbs.

Anna's medical practice was an extensive one and she was very well respected and sought after as a healer. Many of her patients referred to her as Doctor Anna. The acclaim for Anna continued to grow. About this time there was a deadly sickness known as Milksick. It occurred in late summer and early fall each year. Many people and cows sickened from the disease and died. No one knew the cause or the cure. Many of the superstitious, backwoods folk of the area believed that the sickness was caused by the magic potions of witches. Anna, being much more educated than the average person at the time, did not believe in witches. A local Indian squaw and she set out to find the remedy for this deadly disease. They believed that it was caused by something that the cows were eating. After many weeks of observing cattle, Anna and the Indian squaw observed the cows eating White Snakeroot and determined that this was the cause of the mysterious disease. Armed with this knowledge, men scoured the woods and pastures on a mission to eradicate the weed. The mysterious and deadly Milkweed disease was defeated.

Soon after Anna discovered the cause of the Milkweed sickness, her husband died of pneumonia. Several years later, Anna married a ne'er-do-well timber thief by the name of Eson Bigsby. He had only married Anna for the vast amount of money he thought she had. One dark and stormy night, as Anna was going to call on a patient, Eson and some of his criminal buddies seized her and bound her in chains. They then pushed her off a cliff and set fire to the woods. Anna got caught in tree branches during her fall from the cliff. A storm quickly brewed up and the torrential rain fall drenched the flames. Anna was saved from the flames, managed to free herself from the chains, climbed down from the tree and made good her escape.

There is a cave near Rock Creek in Hooven Hollow that is known as Bixby Cave. Legend has it that this cave is the hiding place of Anna Bixby's fortune. Many intrepid souls have sought to find the missing gold and silver coins. While no one has admitted to finding the Bigsby treasure, many have reported weird happenings in and around the cave. Strange, glowing balls of light have been sighted in the area. These lights are said to be a lantern held by the ghost of Dr. Anna Bigsby as she goes about her rounds to guard her treasure and to tend to her beloved sick and injured patients.

Good Hope Church Cemetery

Good Hope Cemetery is located off Karbers Ridge Blacktop in Hardin County. There have been numerous reports of paranormal activity at this location that include ghosts, weird lights and strange noises. The cemetery is considered to be very haunted.

A headless ghost with chains around his neck has been seen walking along the road in front of the cemetery. There is also a mysterious nameless horror that stalks night time visitor to the cemetery. Many glowing balls of light have been observed in the cemetery and near the church.

One man reported that he and two friends decided to spend the night in the cemetery and church grounds just to see for themselves what type of paranormal activity they would encounter. During the night, two things happened that they could not explain. First, they heard strange hollow sounds of rapping on wood coming from a location near the center of the cemetery and then a deep snarling growl that came from the woods next to the church.

Courtney Barnard McKinley states,

> *"People have experienced strange things there such as "'shadows"'.' One thing that creeped me out once was when I was standing there late evening by myself (went to visit for memorial day since I was out of town when the rest of my family went and I didn't wanna leave it out) and it was starting to get dark. I am so certain I heard footsteps behind me several times... I would turn around quickly and no one was there. It gave me chills. I haven't been back alone since. It really scared me. I've also heard stories of people seeing apparitions there, following them and then they disappeared. Along with the usual stories of unknown noises, etc. I believe there's definitely something to it, along with every other cemetery. There's just too much thickness in the air there for there not to be something going on."*

No one knows for sure what may be causing the paranormal events at Good Hope Church Cemetery, and most likely never will.

Illinois Iron Furnace

According to legend, before the Civil War slaves were used to fill the Illinois Iron Furnace with iron ore and charcoal to make pig iron. During one very hot day, one of the slaves was overcome by the intolerable white hot heat from the top of the furnace and fell head first into the inferno and was burnt to ash. It is said that the spirit of this unfortunate slave would be see in and around the old iron furnace screaming in agony for many years afterwards. The Illinois Iron Furnace is located in the Shawnee National Forest near Elizabethtown, Illinois. It is the only remaining iron furnace structure in Illinois.

The Illinois Iron Furnace was built in 1837. Some of the pig iron smelted there was used at the Mound City Naval Shipyards to clad the gunboats they built. The furnace fell into disuse in 1861. It worked sporadically throughout the 1870's and 1880's. Then, in the 1930's, members of the Civilian Conservation Corps dismantled most of the furnace. The stones were used to build the embankments of the Hog Creek Thief Bridge, so what stands today was rebuilt in 1967.

Jackson County

Daniel Harmon Brush

On February 10, 1890, Daniel Brush was in his study writing his memoirs. The property outside his window was being cleared for Brush School. He left his writing to offer assistance in removing a tree. He was holding one of the ropes but made the mistake of tying it around his waist. When the tree fell, he was catapulted into the air and slammed into the ground. Resulting injuries caused his death. Brush School burned in the 1970's. In 1982, its remnants were removed and the Carbondale Public Library now stands on the site. There have been sightings of an older gruff man dressed in 1890's clothing wandering around the grounds of the Carbondale Public Library. Patrons of the library have reported that books have mysteriously flown off the shelves as they passed by. Could this be the ghost of Daniel Brush come back to haunt the land he lived and died on?

John A. Logan – Confederate Soldier?

While doing some research at the Marion Carnage Library genealogy section we came across some evidence that General John A. Logan of Civil War and southern Illinois fame actually commanded a Confederate Army unit at the beginning of the Civil War. In one heated battle, a member of the Union Army captured John A. Logan's horse. Logan is most famous for organizing the 31st Illinois Volunteer Infantry in southern Illinois and leading this Union Army unit to many victories. Very few in southern Illinois are aware of General Logan's early Confederate service.

Mystery of the Woodlawn Sarcophagus

Located on the east side of a hill at Woodlawn Cemetery in Carbondale, Illinois, there is a stone sarcophagus raised a few feet above the ground. The sarcophagus and the two pedestals it rests on were carved from Boskeydell sandstone. Any inscriptions on the stone have long since been obliterated by the ravages of time.

There are several stories about who the sarcophagus contains. The best known and most believable one to me is that it contains the remains of a

Confederate woman from Vicksburg, Mississippi, who moved to Carbondale with her husband shortly after the Civil War. She hated the Union so much that she made her husband promise never to bury her in Union soil. When she died, the promise was kept by raising the sarcophagus a few feet above the ground. Some people believe that this was done simply because the ground was too hard to dig the grave to bury the woman.

One other version involves Lieutenant Colonel John Mills, a Union soldier who died just after the Civil War. The Colonel's family sealed him in the sarcophagus. Upon learning that a Confederate soldier was to be buried in the cemetery, the family removed the Colonel's body, leaving the sarcophagus empty. Personally, I do not believe this version because the sarcophagus is very short and doubt it could accommodate a full size man.

Oakland Cemetery

Oakland Cemetery is located on North Oakland Street in Carbondale. The cemetery is known for various supernatural happenings. Some of the creepy things that have been reported there include the apparition of a beautiful young lady in a flowing white gown that makes her nocturnal rounds on the east side of the cemetery. There is a mausoleum whose doors mysteriously unlock from time to time seemingly to allow the unaware or foolhardy to enter. Wispy vapors and glowing balls of light have been reported along the north side on the cemetery near where the railroad tracks used to run by. Strange cryptozoological creatures have also been spotted along the path where the railroad tracks used to run.

There is an old mausoleum in Oakland Cemetery in Carbondale that appears to be illuminated from the inside when viewed from Oakland Street at nighttime. However, when you approach the mausoleum, the "lights" mysteriously vanish. We decided to investigate the strange happenings one evening. The mausoleum has massive bronze and glass doors at the front and a stained glass window on the back. While standing at the front doors and peering through the window at the crypts, we heard an unearthly "whirring" sound that seemed to surround us. There was no wind or anything nearby that could have made the sound. In fact, the entire cemetery was deathly quiet. At the base of the mausoleum I noticed some "vents."

I decided to shine my flashlight in the vent to see what was behind the screen. I was surprised to see a casket a couple of feet inside. I called my wife over to look inside and just as she did, she started coughing and gagging and almost vomited. I jokingly told her that she must have been a victim of "corpse gas." We walked back to the truck so my wife could recover from whatever had made her sick. While driving away from the mausoleum, something "unseen" opened the passenger door of the truck. Even though it was a very warm evening the temperature seemed to drop about 20 degrees as soon as the door was flung open. What is the source of the mystery light? What was the strange "whirring" noise? What was the "corpse gas?" Who or what opened the door of the truck? The investigation continues.

1888 Train Wreck

Lisa, one of our lead investigators, found some interesting information while conducting research at the Carbondale Public Library. On March 31, 1888 there was a horrific train wreck near Oakland Cemetery in Carbondale, Illinois. Further research revealed that the

ICRR was cited for unsafe conditions less than 2 weeks prior to the train wreck.

John Chapman, the engineer of the Illinois Central Railroad train was killed in the wreck on Sunday morning, March 31, 1888. He was born in Lincolnshire, England, October 9, 1854 and was aged 33 years, 5 months and 22 days. Funeral Services were held at his residence, Sunday, April 1, at 2 o'clock p.m. by Rev. F. Stolz. Interment at Oakland Cemetery occurred under the auspices of the Masonic Fraternity. The undertaker charged forty dollars for casket and other expenses.

Until the 1990's railroad tracks ran along the northern boundary of Oakland Cemetery. On many occasions, earth lights have been seen along the tracks. Photographs taken near the north boundary of the cemetery show various wispy vapors among the gravestones. We wonder if the train wreck of March 31, 1888 has anything to do with paranormal sightings at Oakland Cemetery.

Murdered by Unknown Hands

One grave in Carbondale's Oakland Cemetery had mystified the members of the Little Egypt Ghost Society for quite some time. It was the grave of Thelma Wise, age 26, who according to her grave stone was "Murdered by Unknown Hands."

Just who was Thelma Wise and what really happened to her? After extensive research, we discovered that she was not murdered. According to the Coroner's

Certificate of Death, she committed suicide. Many years ago there was a social and religious stigma attached to suicide, but not murder. We think it was the family's way of covering up a tragic family secret.

There have been sightings of a spectral lady in a long, white, flowing gown that seems to glide among the grave stones in the area where Thelma Wise is buried. Is it possible that this is the spirit of Thelma who is remorseful over taking her own life and the anguish that it caused her family?

The name on this Coroner's Certificate of Death is THELMA MASON. This was corrected to read THELMA WISE. (See next photo)

The cause of death was suicide by strangulation due to hanging, not "murder by unknown hands" as carved on her grave stone. (See photo)

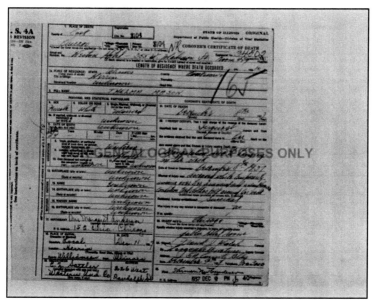

This is the supplemental report on the Coroner's Certificate of Death correcting the record to read THELMA WISE.

(See photo. 'It is difficult to read since 'FOR GENEALOGICAL PURPOSES ONLY' is printed over it)

The Unknowns of Oakland Cemetery

The old and musty record books that are maintained in the cemetery Sexton's office hold many interesting and sometimes mysterious facts. The oldest recorded burial at Oakland Cemetery in Carbondale is that of James Roberts who was buried in what is now Block 22, Lot 20, and Space 5 on March 31, 1863. The oldest known gravestone at Oakland Cemetery is that of Henry G. Hamilton located in Block 30, Lot 6, and Space 1. The interesting and mysterious fact about this burial is that there is no body buried there. Cemetery workers have probed all around the gravestone without any indication of anything buried there. They even used dowsing rods to locate the body with negative results. The gravestone was moved to its present location from some unknown site.

Until the 1940s, Oakland Cemetery was segregated. The record books contain the names and locations of people buried there under the headings of "White People" and "Colored People." Sections 1, 2, 3, 4, 5 and 6 were reserved for "Colored People." The old records were written on various scraps of paper including a page off a 1941 calendar. A hand drawn map indicated locations of graves with markings such as "next to red oak tree." The cemetery workers say that the trees used as landmarks are no longer there and the graves are now missing.

The Illinois Central Railroad used to run along the north side of Oakland Cemetery. Back in the steam train days, whenever a transient died on the train, the bodies were wrapped in a sheet or tarp. When the trains passed Oakland Cemetery, the train slowed down and the bodies were unceremoniously dumped off the train into the cemetery and they would be buried the next morning. Blocks 80, 81 and 82 became the Potter's Field burial site for these transients. Block 80 contains 115 burials, but only 12 of them are marked. If you visit this section after a heavy snowfall, you can see the depressions in the ground where many of the missing graves are located.

Oakland Cemetery is known for various earth lights and swirling mists throughout its north side. Could these mysterious lights and mists be the spirits of the unknown transient dead from the old-time steam trains?

The Flipping Cemetery

Located between Carbondale and Desoto is a small country cemetery that has long been known for strange happenings late at night. Local legend says that on certain nights the cemetery appears to "flip" into a mirror image of itself. One night we decided to go there after I got off work at 11:30pm. We brought along our ghost hunting kit with EMF meters, EVP recorders and pyrometers. We turned onto the lonely country lane that the cemetery is located on and parked our car in front of the main gate. There was a full moon that night and we were able to get a good view of the various gravestones.

We waited in the silence of the moonbeams for the cemetery to "flip"," and not a "flipping" thing happened. We did however get some high readings on our EMF meters just in front of the main gate. After waiting several minutes, we went back to the car and sat for a while longer. After about 5 minutes, I looked in the rear view mirror and noticed a tall, thin smoky mist like entity standing at the rear bumper of our car. Right at this moment our EMF meters detected a strong electromagnetic field. As we sat there and watched the figure, it began to move to the passenger side of the car.

The smoky mist began to evaporate into thin air as it approached the passenger door. We left the area later with nothing additional to report. When we got back to Carbondale we pulled into a lighted parking lot and I got out of the car. When I walked to the rear of our car, I noticed that there were two dusty hand prints on my otherwise clean car. These hand prints corresponded exactly with where the entity was standing. It was as if someone or something had risen out of a grave and left its mark. Normally, hand prints are left on a "dusty" car. It was the exact opposite in this case. My car was clean and the hand prints were dusty. Could this be an effect of the "flipping" cemetery with the hand prints being the reverse of what they should have been?

House on West College Street

John Carter (names have been changed to protect privacy) killed himself in his home on W. College St., Carbondale. The previous year Carter's mother died. Carter never married and lived all his life with his mother. Upon the mother's death, Carter's siblings got a court order evicting Carter from the only home he had known. The siblings only cared about the money they would get from the sale of the home (less than $5,000) and caring little where their brother would go. Before killing himself, he told a friend: "I'm not going to leave this place." Carter was to be evicted from the home on W. College Street by police acting on a court order.

Nine officers went to the home to force Carter out. They broke into the locked house and found Carter dead of a gunshot wound. He apparently shot himself several days prior. Carter was sitting in a chair in his bedroom. The wound under his chin apparently was inflicted by the .410 gauge shotgun nearby. The old, single-shot gun had been fired once. He apparently killed himself rather than be forced from the house he refused to leave. When the court proceedings to evict were begun, Carter told a friend: "I'm not going to leave this place." His ghost never did leave and still haunts the house to this day. He is buried in Oakland Cemetery.

1925 Boskydell Train Wreck

In 1925, an Illinois Central train wrecked in what is now the ghost town of Boskydell, Illinois just south of Carbondale. A hobo, who had hitched a ride on the train, had his legs trapped between two of the wrecked train cars. A crowd quickly gathered and watched as the man screamed in agony. No one made an attempt to move the train cars to free the man because they believed it would kill him. After a long delay, a doctor who had been called from Carbondale arrived at the wreck. By lantern light, the doctor opened his black leather medical bag and retrieved his amputation saw and knife. After a few quick slices with the knife, the amputation saw finished the job. The man's legs were tossed to the side of the railroad tracks. The nearly unconscious hobo died on the way to the hospital in Carbondale. On some nights people claim to have seen a strange glowing light along the railroad tracks and tell of the blood curdling screams under a full moon. Is this a residual haunting of those tragic events of the train wreck?

WSIU-TV Interview with Little Egypt Ghost Society

Danielle, a reporter for WSIU-TV, was looking for an interesting news story when she came across the Little Egypt Ghost Society website on Facebook. Intrigued, she made contact with our ghost hunter club and asked if we would consent to an interview. Of course, the answer was a resounding "yes!" A date was decided on when she could interview the club officers.

The interview was conducted with co-founders Bruce and Lisa Cline. During the interview, we were asked what got us interested in ghost hunting and what some of the most interesting encounters were. After that a demonstration was made of all the official Little Egypt Ghost Society equipment. Danielle's interest was now at an all-time high. She asked if she could go on a ghost hunt with our group and film it. Once again the answer was, "yes!"

Our group had been asked to conduct a paranormal investigation of an old two-story house on North Almond Street in Carbondale. The upstairs apartment in the house was shared by Josh, his girlfriend and another female roommate. They stated that the house was over 100 years old and had once stood on the land where Crab Orchard Lake is now located. When work on the lake was started in 1936, it was decided to move the house to Carbondale.

Josh said that he found an old guitar in the attic of the house and decided to add it to his collection of vintage guitars. He hung the old guitar on the wall near some of the others. Each night, the old guitar would fall off the nail that held it up. No matter how many times he re-hung it, it would always fall off the nail. He also said that he and his girlfriend and roommate would hear sounds of a small animal in the hallway by the bedrooms and would see the shadow of it on the walls. This in itself was not strange except for the fact that they had no pets in the house!

We all agreed on a date for the TV crew to film the investigation. After the investigators and TV crew arrived at the house introductions were made and the background of the strange happenings was made known to all present. Danielle checked all of the equipment to be used for the investigation to make sure that the batteries were fresh and that everything was in good working order. Just as we went into the room where the guitar had been falling off the wall, the TV camera stopped working.

Danielle rechecked her equipment and could find no logical reason why it would not work. I explained to her that sometimes during a paranormal investigation, electronic equipment would fail whenever spirit activity was nearby. Fortunately, I had my SONY NightShot Camcorder with infrared lighting enabling us to continue to film the investigation. We took several temperature readings with our pyrometers and Kestrel Weather Monitor and found an area in the back bedroom that had a temperature drop of 14 degrees in one small area near the center of the room.

The dowsing rods we were using would cross at exactly the same spot. After two hours, we decided to end the investigation. Just as soon as we turned on all the lights, Danielle's TV camera mysteriously started working again. It seemed like whatever spirits were in the house did not want her to document what was going on.

We did not see any guitars flying thru the air and did not hear or see the spectral animals. All we had to show for our efforts was one cold spot, crossed dowsing rods, a TV camera that mysteriously stopped working and one very scared TV reporter.

Sunset Haven

One of the creepiest and mysterious buildings in Carbondale is the Vivarium Annex, also known as Building 207, located at Sunset Haven. Many people have mistakenly called it "the Insane Asylum." Originally, it was the Jackson County Poor Farm. It became a home for the destitute, mentally ill and severely retarded. In the 1940's its name was changed to Sunset Haven and converted into a nursing home. In 1957 Southern Illinois University purchased the property, changed its name to

Building 207 and used the building and surrounding land for agricultural programs.

Sunset Haven has long been known as one of the major haunted spots in Carbondale. It is well known for paranormal activity such as disembodied voices, doors that open and then slam on their own accord, sounds of moaning, cries, chains being dragged, animal sounds, cold spots, lights that turn on and off as well as the creepy feeling of being watched by unseen eyes.

The Little Egypt Ghost Society was intrigued by the history, mystery and hauntings of Sunset Haven. It was decided that this was one location that we needed to investigate. We contacted a reporter with the Daily Egyptian Newspaper at S.I.U. to see if she could help obtain official permission from S.I.U. for us to go there. After negotiations with authorities at S.I.U., we finally had the long sought after permission.

Just hours before our scheduled walk thru, the Chief of the Southern Illinois University Police Department denied all access to the property. Members of the Little Egypt Ghost Society investigation team along with a reporter from the Daily Egyptian went to the S.I.U. Police Dept to speak with the chief of police. We were denied access to the chief and met with the director of the department of public safety instead. We once again asked permission to conduct the investigation stating that Sunset Haven had a reputation of being haunted and that we wanted to check it out for ourselves.

At that point, the director expressed his skepticism at the reputation of the location as being haunted. I then produced copies of books by three of my favorite authors, Michael Kleen, Troy Taylor, and Jim Jung, all of which contained stories about Sunset Haven and the reputed hauntings that occur there. I went on to explain that there are several websites devoted to the hauntings of Sunset Haven. The director then stated that the location was too dangerous for us to be there and my reply was, "why then, do S.I.U. Army ROTC and the Carbondale and S.I.U. Police Departments conduct tactical exercises there?" He was at a loss for words and just reiterated that it the chief's decision not to allow us access.

The bottom line was that ghost hunters and paranormal investigators are "persona non grata" at Sunset Haven in Carbondale. The area is patrolled by police on a regular basis and all trespassers will be arrested on sight.

All this secrecy makes us wonder...just what is S.I.U. trying to hide?

Got REIKI?

Little Egypt Ghost Society was recently recalled to a home in Carbondale, Illinois whose owners have been troubled by the spirit of a man named "Sam L." who was a WWII veteran and previous owner of the house. The couple was so terrified of unexplained sounds, objects moving, and unexpected temperature changes in their bedroom that they were forced to sleep on couches in the living room. The family dog would lie on his back and act as if someone was rubbing his belly. The couple was terrified and wanted the spirit GONE! Rich McLevich, our Reiki Master and Kale Meggs, our Historical Researcher went to the house to try to determine what was causing the disturbances.

We had previously investigated this home, finding various unexplained EMF spikes and temperature changes in certain locations of the home. Rick was able to use his Reiki skills to make contact with the spirit of "Sam." There had been numerous break-ins at the home and "Sam" was concerned for the safety of the couple who lived there. "Sam" indicated that Rick and Kale should go to certain locations outside the house to view vulnerable areas that burglars could use to gain access to the home. After that, "Sam" communicated that everyone should go back inside the house to view a painting of lions.

According to Reiki, everything has a certain energy and power imbedded inside. "Sam" wanted the painting of the lions moved from one wall to a location near the bedroom door. He said the energy from the lion painting would help protect the occupants and possessions in the house. Rick and Kale then performed a smudging with white sage and Reiki Protection on the house to clear any negative energy from the home. After further communication with "Sam," it was determined that he was not a threat to the safety or wellbeing of the couple living in the home. "Sam" was in fact their protector. The couple was very relieved to learn this and is now happily living with the spirit of "Sam."

The Old Carbondale Train Depot

Carbondale Main Street asked the Little Egypt Ghost Society to conduct a ghost hunt at the old Carbondale Train Depot as one of their Halloween events. Several months prior, we had conducted an initial investigation of this historic location.

There were 12 people present for our Halloween ghost hunt at the old train depot. Just before we started the EVP session, the PX device we were using said "LIGHT" and then the lights in the office went off. No one was in the office at the time. We used our short list (25 questions) of questions for the EVP session in the office where the lights went out. We got responses to a couple of the questions, but what they were will have to be determined through further analysis. During one of the EVP responses, several members of the group stated they heard something "strange" and the floor felt like it was vibrating the way it would if a train was passing by. No trains passed the station at any time during the EVP session.

The PX device was silent for over an hour until just before our EVP session when it said a few things that made sense in the context of where we were and what was going on.

There have been reported sightings of passengers dressed in clothes from the 1880s boarding a train at the Old Carbondale Train Depot. The sightings are an example of residual ghost activity, the kind normally found in Carbondale, in which spirits are just going on with their everyday lives. In residual ghost activity, they do not realize they are dead, and they are not really paying any attention to the outside world. As far as they are aware, it is still 1882.

The Old Carbondale Train Station was constructed by the Illinois Central Railroad (ICRR) in 1903. The depot on Carbondale's Town Square served as the city's primary point of departure and arrival well into the 1940s.

The depot was constructed of brick and limestone with a slate roof at a cost of $15,900 and contained baggage rooms, ticket and telegraph offices, and waiting rooms.

The first addition, the Van Noy Lunch Room Building, was completed in 1905. It stood about 40 feet north of the depot. In 1925, a mail room enclosure measuring 20 feet by 40 feet was added to the depot. In 1930, the baggage room at the north end of the building was expanded. The mail enclosure was widened at this time as well, and the separate men's and women's waiting areas were remodeled to provide general waiting and depot offices. A total of $4,100 was spent on these 1930 additions.

It is very common for batteries and other electrical items to be drained of power during paranormal investigations. As we were starting our EVP session trying to make contact with "Allen," all the power in the train depot went off. In fact, all the power in the west side of Carbondale went off at that same time. We continued our EVP session and other activities for some time when we decided to call it a night and pack up our equipment. After we stowed all our equipment and made preparations to leave, the power came back on in the main office area where we were standing. The alarm system should have sounded off 30 seconds after the power was restored, but did not. The rep from Carbondale Main Street said that really creeped her out.

At least we warned her that something like this would probably happen.

The Sound Core Ghosts

This single-story commercial building, which is divided into two stores, has been the site of numerous businesses since its original construction in the 1890's. A circa 1900 photograph reveals the building originally exhibited an elaborate stamped metal façade.

That photograph also shows the south half of the building was occupied by Booney Furniture & Undertakers and the north half contained the Peak & Storm grocery store. Between 1906 and 1913, the original metal surface was removed and the façade rebricked. A c. 1912 photograph shows the building's elaborate pressed tin façade removed and a modest brick façade in its place.

At that time, the south half of the building housed the Book Store, and the north half contained the "E Five 7 Ten Cent Store." By the late 1930's, the building's façade had been covered yet again with glazed tile. A c. 1940 photograph revels the north half of the building housed the "Carbondale Café," which displayed a large, overhanging sign advertising the café's "candy and sodas." Both buildings appear to have been rebricked again in the 1950's and 60's.

Today, this building is considered haunted by several people. Employees and customers of Sound Core have reported unexplained cold spots in certain areas of the building along with the feeling of being watched by unseen eyes. Some females have stated that "something" touched them when no one was nearby. It is believed that these paranormal events date back to the days when this building was a funeral home. The son of the funeral home owner was a spoiled playboy who liked ladies, booze and money. On one summer day, the owner's son was partying at Giant City Park with some lady friends. The liquor was flowing freely and the partiers became quite drunk. While hiking along one of the bluffs, the young man fell to his death. His dead body was brought back to the funeral home that his family owned for embalming and the funeral. It is believed that his spirit never left the building.

Murphysboro Mud Monster

Contrary to published accounts by famous cryptozoologists and other so-called experts, the "Big Muddy Monster," aka "Murphysboro Mud Monster," is a fabricated hoax. How do we know? We know it to be a fact because we are personally acquainted with the perpetrator of the hoax. "Willy" has revealed to us the complete and true details of what the "mud monster" was and how he did it. Complete details are on file in the archives of the Little Egypt Ghost Society.

What follows is the generally accepted account of the Big Muddy Monster.

The first recorded sighting of the Big Muddy Monster took place on June 25, 1973, near Murphysboro, Illinois. According to the Murphysboro Police Department, the Big Muddy Monster remains one of two open cases in the history of the department. Two visitors to Riverside Park in Murphysboro were parked in a car when they heard a loud screaming sound in the wooded area and observed a large creature approximately 7 feet tall. The creature appeared to have light-colored hair matted with mud. The creature appeared to be walking on two legs and was proceeding toward their car.

Police searched the area with flashlights and spotted tracks in the mud approximately 3 to 4 inches deep, 10 to 12 inches long, and 3 inches wide. While officers were searching the area they reported hearing another scream coming from the woods. The next night, two teenagers sitting on a porch reported a tall, white-haired, hairy creature in a field just to the edge of the woods. Using a police dog, officers followed the creature making note of a discernable foul smell and slime on the branches. The dog tracked the creature to an empty barn.

This is the real story:

On a warm summer night in June of 1973, two young lovers came face to face with a creature that has baffled cryptozoologists for almost 40 years. On that fateful night, the young couple was "parking" at Riverside Park alongside the Big Muddy River in Murphysboro,

Illinois. As they were watching the stars, they were startled by some movement they saw in the woods next to the river. As they strained their eyes in the darkness to see what it was, a 7 foot tall creature covered in mud matted fur emerged from the woods. Just as they were nearly overcome by an overpowering stench, they heard a blood curdling scream come from the creature that was walking erect like a man.

The young couple hurriedly started their car and went straight to the Murphysboro Police Department to report what had happened. Police were dispatched to Riverside Park and the surrounding area to search for the creature. When they arrived, all they found were some very fresh and very large footprints made by an unknown creature. While at the scene the police reported hearing a bellowing scream come from the woods.

The Jackson County Sheriff Department sent a K-9 unit in hopes of locating the creature. The police dog tracked whatever it was to a barn, but the dog refused to enter it. Once again there was an overpowering stench in the area.

The Big Muddy Monster is an open police case in Murphysboro to this day because they just don't know what it was.

The hoax was perpetrated by "Willie" (His real name is in the case files of the Little Egypt Ghost Society) and two of his associates. Willie is a science fiction, paranormal and zombie fanatic. He is extremely skilled in theatrical makeup, costume design and film making. In early summer of 1973, Willie got together with his associates and they decided it would be great fun to create a large, hairy monster costume to frighten the locals who used Riverside Park as a "lover's lane." They put together a costume that was over 6 feet tall and covered it with fur that was heavily matted with mud from the river bank. They left out no detail and even made realistic, oversized feet for the costume that would leave credible footprints. Next they went to their garage lab and concocted a batch of "Eau de Sasquatch" stink juice to go alone with the prank.

The night of June 25, 1973 at Riverside Park in Murphysboro was the only time that Willie and his friends performed this elaborate hoax. Willie put on the mud monster costume while his associates stood ready with the Eau de Sasquatch stink juice. After all of the preparations were made, they waited in the woods for some "parkers" to show up. Shortly before midnight their preparations paid off as a young couple drove to a secluded spot nearby. After waiting a short time, the 'mud monster" made his presence known with grunting and loud bellowing screams, the associates quickly sprayed the area with the stink juice. Much to the delight of Willie and his associates, the young couple quickly left the park with their car tires squealing.

It seems that people liked the story about the monster and there was a snowball effect causing various other "sightings" of the Big Muddy Monster, but no further evidence of its existence was ever found. Due to all of the police and public attention that the "monster" sighting received, Willie and his associates were afraid that they would get into serious trouble if they were ever found out (Willie is to this day, nearly 40 years later, fearful and reluctant to talk about the hoax).

A Murder, a Hanging and a Haunting

It was a hot, muggy day in Murphysboro, Illinois on July 30, 1915. Lizzy Martin, the wife of prominent Murphysboro attorney, James Martin, was found brutally murdered in her home on North Ninth Street. She had been savagely beaten on her head and upper body. The only suspect in this horrendous crime was the Martin's live-in handyman, a negro by the name of Joe DeBerry. At first, he denied killing Mrs. Martin. After intense questioning by the Jackson County Sheriff, DeBerry confessed to bludgeoning Mrs. Martin with a fireplace poker. The reason for this crime was never clear. Some say he had been accused of stealing and had been caught by Mrs. Martin. Others said that he killed her because she refused to give him 50 cents for a haircut.

One month after the murder, DeBerry was found guilty and sentenced to death by hanging. October 16, 1915 was the day of the execution. The Murphysboro Daily Independent newspaper reported that "fog hung over the city like a cloak of death." Jackson County Sheriff James White deputized 2,000 citizens of Murphysboro so that all could obtain a good view of the hanging. Executions were very good for business in Murphysboro. Hotels, restaurants and shops were all crowded with customers. The entire downtown had a carnival atmosphere to it.

DeBerry was hung on the same scaffold that was used to hang Charlie Birger several years later. Once the trap door was sprung, it took De Berry 16 minutes to die.

After the death of Lizzy's husband, James, rumors began to circulate that the majestic Victorian home that they had lived and died in was haunted. During the 1940s

71

a fire destroyed the top portion of the stately Victorian home that the Martins once lived in. The two-story Victorian home was remodeled into a one story bungalow. Starting in the late 1940s, occupants of the house would report mysterious sounds. It is not known if the strange creaks and other noises were due to the brutal murder that took place there or if it was the result of extensive remodeling that perhaps the spirits of the Martin's did not approve of. Many residual hauntings have been reported wherever there was a tragic event or remodeling of an older structure.

The Cottonwood Tree

The mid 1800s were violent times for southern Illinois and 1874 would be one of those violent years. Early spring brought death to an unknown black man who was accused of robbing, raping and murdering a white woman in Carbondale, Illinois. The man was quickly arrested and locked up in the Jackson County jail in Murphysboro.

The public was outraged at this heinous crime. An angry mob of about 200 men and women gathered around the jail. When it became evident that the Sheriff and Jailer were not at their post, the mob broke down the doors to the jail and forcefully removed the black man. The crowd, hell bent for leather and wanting revenge, carried the frightened prisoner to a site near the old Mt. Carbon Bridge on the Big Muddy River just east of town. They hastily hurled a short rope over a high branch of a cottonwood tree and Granny Patchett, a prominent lady in Murphysboro was given the "honor" of placing the noose around the black man's neck. Many referred to her as "good old Granny Patchett."

The Murphysboro Daily Independent newspaper reported that "the best people of Murphysboro were in the lynching party, and no one was arrested, though the state's attorney made some fuss about it." After the black man had been left hanging overnight, a Murphysboro doctor cut him down and took the body to his office where he removed all the flesh. The doctor then reassembled the skeleton and displayed it in his medical office for many years. The whereabouts of the skeleton is a closely guarded secret to this day.

Thus is the story of the only recorded lynching in Jackson County, Illinois. Only the footings of the Mt. Carbon Bridge remain today and the cottonwood tree has long since been swept away by floods along the Big Muddy River. Several fishermen along this stretch of the Big Muddy River report mournful cries and wispy vaporous forms along the river banks. Could this be the spectral replay of a ghostly lynching that took place there almost 140 years ago?

The Ghosts of Devils Backbone and Grand Tower

French priests discovered Tower Rock near the Missouri side of the Mississippi River in 1698. The local Indians believed that evil spirits lived on Tower Rock. To dispel the fears of the Indians, the priests erected a wooden cross on top of of the rock to show that the Christian faith was stronger than any evil. This area of the Mississippi River is thought to contain evil spirits. This is reflected by the various names associated with landmarks nearby; Devil's Backbone, Devil's Bake Oven and Devil's tea Table.

One legend of the area is about an Indian brave named Woncasta and the tribal chief's daughter named YaRohNia. The two of them were in love, but the chief had promised his daughter's hand in marriage to a brave of another tribe named YeWongAte. The two braves fought over the girl until a medicine man appeared. To settle the dispute, the medicine man instructed the two braves to climb to the top of Tower Rock and smoke the medicine pipe. Whoever blew the smoke the highest would win the girl.

YeWongAte won the contest and was entitled to the girl. Unbeknownst to everyone, the girl had observed what had happened. She was grief stricken, and instead of going with the brave that had won her, she leapt off the top of Tower Rock, falling 100 feet to her death in the river below. Woncasta was also grief stricken. He took the plunge and followed the girl he loved in death.

During the full moon, passersby have purported the sight of the two lovers united in death with smiles of happiness and contentment on their faces.

A Tragic Wedding

A very tragic wedding occurred at Grand Tower, Illinois on April 9, 1839. The wedding party crossed the river to hold the ceremony on top of Tower Rock. After the ceremony, the wedding party was leaving Tower Rock, when their boat got caught in a whirlpool. The only survivor was a slave. On the same day, the bridegroom's niece was born. For her twentieth birthday on April 9, 1859, a party was held on Tower Rock and the slave who survived the whirlpool was her special guest. During the party the doomed original wedding party appeared to rise from the depths of the Mississippi River and the priest handed the niece a parchment scroll.

The ghostly wedding party then sank back into the river without speaking a word. The parchments predicted a great war in which families would be torn apart and bring great sadness. Two years later, the Civil War began. One of the niece's brothers enlisted with the Union Army and another brother joined the Confederate Army. During a battle in Missouri the Union brother killed Confederate brother, thus fulfilling the prophecy.

The Hundley House

J. Charles Hundley and his wife Luella built the Hundley House in Carbondale in 1907. Hundley was a very prosperous businessman and one time mayor of Carbondale. Just 2 weeks before Christmas in 1928, J. Charles Hundley was shot in the head as he was getting ready for bed in his 2nd floor bedroom on the northeast corner of the house. 'It is believed that his killer was hiding behind the headboard of the bed that sat at an angle in the bedroom. Luella Hundley was shot in kitchen area near the rear of the house. Both Hundleys were shot with a .45 caliber handgun. The killer escaped without a trace and was never found.

Many people, including the police, suspected J. C. Hundley's son from a previous marriage, Victor, as the murderer. In the weeks before the murder, J. C. Hundley and Victor had dissolved a mining contract they held. Victor was to inherit $300,000 from Luella upon her death. It seemed that Victor had much to gain with J. C. and Luella out of the way. Police searched Victor's house and found a shirt and coat covered with bloodstains. Victor claimed that the blood was from one of his hunting expeditions. Lab tests conducted in St. Louis proved that the blood was not human. The Hundley murder remains unsolved to this day.

Dan Jones is the current owner of Hundley House. He operates it as a bed and breakfast. We met with Dan to discuss the Hundley murders and reports of paranormal activity at the house.

Dan has a theory that the Hundley's daughter, not son, was the actual murder. She had the motive, opportunity and possibly the means to do it. He shared some of his personal experiences with us. Dan said that the front porch swing would move without anyone being in or near it. At first he thought it might be the wind causing the motion, but one evening when the swing started moving, he went on the front porch to investigate and discovered that there was no wind what-so-ever. The air was dead calm. On various occasions he said that the computer in the office area would start doing weird things. The computer would turn on by itself and obscene words would start to appear on the computer screen.

Previous residents and visitors to the Hundley House would report strange sounds throughout the house and feelings like someone unseen was in the room with them. One of the creepier areas is the rear stairway near where Luella was shot. People have reported hearing the sound of the wooden stairway creaking, when no one was on the stairs. A .45 caliber bullet hole can still be seen on this stairway. It was made by one of the bullets that passed through Luella Hundley's body the night of the murder.

Southern Illinois University at Carbondale and its Ghosts

Southern Illinois University was founded in 1869 as a teachers college. The first class at S.I.U. had only 143 students. Over the years, S.I.U. attracted more and more people seeking a higher education and now boasts over 20,000 students. According to Scott Thorne, owner of Castle Perilous Games and local ghost historian, S.I.U. (like many colleges and universities) is home to a few resident ghosts.

The Student Center has been reported to be the home of mischievous ghost who moves items, mysteriously closes doors, and causes footsteps to be heard during late night study hours. The Arena which was constructed in 1962 seems to be the host of the same ghosts that inhabit the Student Center.

Faner Hall, constructed in 1971-74 is an enigma. After the anti-war riots at S.I.U. in 1969 and the burning of Old Main by arsonists, it was decided that new building designs would be needed to prevent violent student takeover of classrooms in the future. Faner Hall is without doubt the most confusing building on campus. This massive concrete building was designed with dead-end hallways, multiple entrances, and maze-like construction. It is very easy to get lost in this building and legend has it that shortly after construction was complete a female student got lost in the building late at night and became so frightened by her experience that she died. This may account for the apparition of a girl that lurks the halls of this building. Faner Hall is home to the ghost of a girl wearing a striped shirt and blue jeans. This ghostly girl has been observed on many occasions walking through closed doors and then will vanish. This same phantom has been seen entering various classrooms and then vanishing into thin air.

Shyrock Auditorium, constructed in 1917 is the home for a ghost known as "Henry." Henry is none other than Henry William Shyrock, the 5th president of S.I.U. There is a ghost light near the stage of the auditorium that turns off if its switch is turned on and will turn on is the switch is turned off. At times a "Phantom of the Opera" kind of apparition would be sighted on stage.

Wheeler Hall, Constructed in 1904, has been the scene of poltergeist activity. A woman who was working late one night was attacked by a poltergeist that threw chairs at her.

Anthony Hall is the administrative building for the campus. During the 1960s, one of the female employees suffered a heart attack and died on the job. For many years afterwards, the sounds of typing and file drawers opening and closing were heard in the area where the deceased employee used to work even though no one was sitting at the work area at the time.

Mortuary Science and Funeral Service classroom and lab hosted at least one ghost. We were conducting a ghost hunt training session on the lawn between the

Mortuary Science classroom and Campus Lake on a night in 2008. One of the experiments that we conducted was to use our "Ghost Meters" to make contact with any spirits that might be near. The Ghost Meter is a type of meter that measures electromagnetic fields that may be produced by paranormal activity. It has an analog dial that indicates the level of EMF in milligauss as well as a red flashing light and audible alarm that indicates the intensity of the EMF. Lisa Cline, co-founder of Little Egypt Ghost Society, was able to make contact with the spirit of a female cadaver in the embalming lab. Lisa asked this spirit many questions and got several responses in a special code using the light and sound alarm of the Ghost Meter.

One of the questions that Lisa asked was "how many of you are there in the lab?" The spirit responded with several flashes of the light that would correspond with how many cadavers were in the lab. One of our close friends is an S.I.U. employee and he confirmed that exact number of cadavers that were present in the lab on that night.

The Day a Dead Man hanged a Live Man

Grand Tower, Illinois in the late 1800s was the scene of a very macabre accident in which a dead man hung a live man. The saloon keeper in Grand Tower was a morbidly obese man. In fact, he was the largest man in Jackson County at the time. The town doctor always joked with the saloon keeper that he wanted to bury his body he died. The saloon keeper offered to sell his body for five dollars and the deal was struck.

A short time later, the saloon keeper died and was buried in a very large coffin. The doctor had paid for the body fair and square and was determined to take the body to his medical office for study.

The doctor hired a man to help him dig up the dead man's body. After they dug it up, they realized that the body was too heavy for them to lift out of the grave. They went a got a team of horses and some chain to pull the body out of the grave. The doctor's helper got down in the grave and put the chain around the body. The helper noticed a high fence nearby and looped the other end of the chain over the fence and hitched it to the horse team. As soon as the horses began to pull the chain, it came loose and became wrapped around the helper's neck. The saloon keeper's body was much heavier than the helper's, so the saloon keeper slid back into the grave and the helper was hoisted up on the fence. The live helper was hung by a dead man.

The doctor became frightened that he might be discovered digging up the grave and ran off. The next morning, the helper was found in the cemetery hanging from one end of a chain the dead saloon keeper on the other end of the chain. Many of the town folk said the helper got he deserved for robbing graves.

Johnson County

The Max Creek Vortex

The Max Creek area can be found about half way between Vienna and New Burnside, Illinois. This area is known for tragedy, violence, ghosts and earth lights. Local legend states that a group of early settlers made their home on a bluff above Max Creek. One night the wife of one of the settlers went insane and killed her husband and children. Glowing balls of light can be seen from time to time in the woods near the creek. They are said to be the restless spirits of the murdered family wandering aimlessly seeking the answer to why a loved one would turn on them in such a violent rage.

Max Creek is located near an ancient volcano known as Hicks Dome. Earth lights have been seen all around Hicks Dome. Local Indians would avoid Hicks Dome claiming that it was inhabited by evil spirits. This area has been unpopulated since it was purchased by the National Forest Service in the 1930s. It is now part of the Shawnee National Forest. If you go there some dark and lonely night, you may be fortunate enough to witness the earth lights for yourself.

Madison County

Cahokia Mounds

Cahokia was inhabited from about A.D. 700 to 1400. Built by ancient peoples known as the Mound Builders, Cahokia's original population was thought to have been only about 1,000 until about the 11th Century, when it expanded to tens of thousands.

At its peak from 1,100 to 1,200 A.D., the city covered nearly six square miles and boasted a population of as many as 100,000 people. Houses were arranged in rows around open plazas. Agricultural fields and a number of smaller villages surrounded and supplied the city. The Cahokians were known to have traded with other tribes as far away as Minnesota. The original name of the city is unknown and the inhabitants apparently never utilized writing skills. The name Cahokia is that of an unrelated tribe that was living in the area when the first French explorers arrived in the late 17th century.

These ancient Indians built more than 120 earthen mounds in the city, 109 of which have been recorded and 68 of which are preserved within the site. Many others are thought to have been altered or destroyed by farming and construction. While some are no more than a gentle rise on the land, others reach 100 feet into the sky. Made entirely of earth these ancient people transported the soil on their backs in baskets to the construction sites, most of which show evidence of several construction stages. More than 50 million cubic feet of earth was moved for the construction of the mounds, leaving large depressions called borrow pits, which can still be seen in the area.

Three types of mounds were constructed, the most common of which was a platform mound, thought to have been used as monumental structures for political or religious ceremonies and may have once been topped by large buildings. Conical and ridge top mounds were also constructed for use as burial locations or marking important locations.

At the center of the historical site is the largest earthwork called Monks Mound. At one hundred feet, it is the largest prehistoric earthen mound in North America. The mound is 1,000 feet long, 800 feet wide and comprised of four terraces, each one probably added at different times. An estimated 22 million cubic feet of earth was used to build the mound between the years of 900 and 1,200 A.D. The mound was named for French monks who lived nearby in the early 1800's and was most likely the site where the principal ruler lived, conducted ceremonies, and governed the city. Over the years, the mound has significantly eroded or been damaged by man, so that the original size is now uncertain.

Surrounding Monks Mound and the center of the city was a 2-mile-long stockade with guard towers placed every 70 feet. Thought to have been constructed four different times, each building took nearly 20,000 logs. In addition to defense purposes, the wall acted as a social barrier, separating the elite from the common people. Today, several sections of the stockade have been reconstructed.

Archaeologists have also excavated four, and possibly five, circular sun calendars referred to as Woodhenge. These evenly spaced log posts were utilized to determine the changing seasons, displaying an impressive example of scientific and engineering practices.

The area at Cahokia Mounds that we are primarily interested in is the mysterious Mound #72. Mound #72 is located about one half mile south of Monks Mound and measures 7 ft in height, 140 ft long and 70 feet wide. It covers 3 smaller mounds that were built over high status and sacrificial burials. Some of the more interesting burials are that of a man on a platform of 20,000 shell beads, built in the shape of a falcon. Underneath this man is the skeleton of another man aged in the early 40s and about 6 ft tall. Nearby are 6 burials possibly sacrificed to the man on the beads. One of these skeletons is lying with arms and legs akimbo as if thrown there before death. In another area of the mound is a group of 7 men and women surrounded by many offerings including 2 piles of arrow points; 332 aligned W-NW, and 413 aligned E-SE. 3 more burials are nearby.

21 skeletons are found on a low square platform with at least 13 of them aged between15 and 35 years. On the SE side of the mound there was a 25- 35 year old female wearing a choker with 4 strands of shell disk beads. Next to her was a 25 – 35 year old male wearing a choker with 5 strands of shell disk beads. He was found lying face down. 2 other males were found face down nearby. On the SW side of the mound there are 22 females buried in 2 layers. On the SE side of the mound there are 19 females buried in 2 layers. On another side are 24 females buried in 2 layers. 4 men, aged 20- 45 years with arms interlocked and all missing their heads and hands are in this mound. There are many burial pits surround Mound #72.

Massac County

A Grisly Hobby

In 1898 Dr. Elmo made his own medical skeletons in his barn. Dr. Elmo lived in Samoth which was in Massac County, Illinois. This town no longer exists. Dr. Elmo would boil water to prepare the skeletons. He would have the dead body hanging by the neck in his barn. The clothes would be cut off and the internal organs removed. The flesh would be cut off being careful to preserve the joints. He would bury the guts and then put the dissected body into the kettle of boiling water and quicklime. After the bones were boiled they were bleached white. Dr. Elmo would then assemble the bones into a skeleton for display. It is not known where he obtained the dead bodies.

Fort Massac State Park

Fort Massac, located in Metropolis, was built by the French in 1757 as an outpost to fight off an expected invasion by the British. The original name for the fort was Fort Ascension. Much to the relief of the locals, the invasion never came.

Local legend says that a group of French marines stationed at the fort saw some bears across the river. They quickly gathered up their muskets, knives and canoes and set out to cross the Ohio River in pursuit of the bears. The remaining personnel remained at the fort unarmed and watched the hunting party from the shore.

The French hunting party stealthily positioned themselves so that the bears were trapped between them and the river. The Frenchmen took careful aim and just as they were about to fire they discovered, to their horror, that the bears were in fact Indians that were wearing bear skins as a disguise. The Indians had laid a clever ambush for the Frenchmen. Throwing off their bear skins, the Indians took aim at the Frenchmen at the same moment that another group of Indian warriors charged out of the woods behind the startled French. There were war whoops, screams, yelling and many gunshots. Soon the woods became silent as the last of the Frenchmen were slain. The situation was not any better back at the fort. A group of Indians attacked the unarmed garrison and killed everyone they found there. After these brutal attacks, the French renamed the fort as Fort Massacre which eventually was shortened by the Americans to Fort Massac.

The fort has been considered haunted since 1818. In that year a man by the name of Dillworth was found dead by the river bank. His throat had been cut from ear to ear. The ghost of Dillworth has been seen from time to time along the river bank where he died and at the Visitors Center next to the reconstructed fort. Park employees and visitors have reported sounds of footsteps when no one was there and doors that open and shut by themselves.

Monroe County

Miles Mausoleum

Miles Mausoleum is located on top of Eagle Cliff, overlooking the Mississippi River, near Valmeyer in Monroe County. It was built in 1858 by Stephen W. Miles. At one time, a large marble panel on the right side of the doorway stated that the mausoleum was built by Stephen W. Miles, Esquire, son of the elder Miles, in 1858 as a memorial to the W. Miles family and descendants. It went on to state that the eldest son of each generation was to care for it and to hold it "through this succession in trust for the above family." Another marble panel to the left of the doorway was inscribed with "To the Visitor," with the rest of the inscription unreadable.

Both marble panels are now long gone and mostly forgotten. The Miles name appears above the doorway. Steven Miles would often stand on top of Eagle Cliff and gaze to the horizon and his vast land holdings. He would shout out for all to hear "For miles and miles it is all Miles." Despite grand plans for the upkeep of the tomb, Miles went bankrupt and only 11 of the 56 vaults were ever used. Local lore says that it once housed the bodies of Miles himself, along with his two wives, a few mistresses and a number of servants. Unfortunately, they would not be allowed to rest in peace.

In the early 1960s, the mausoleum was apparently rediscovered where it had been hidden in the enveloping woods. It was broken into, and later visitors said that caskets and bones with dried flesh still clinging to them could be seen everywhere. It was rumored that the tomb had been desecrated in search of the valuable jewels that had been buried with its occupants. A few years later, things continued to get worse. A cult group removed the remaining bodies from their vaults onto the grounds outside, and burned them in their attempt to "raise the dead." As you could probably imagine, stories of ghostly encounters at this site have been numerous and continue to the present.

Perry County

Beacoup Creek

In 1880, the Beacoup Creek in Perry County, Illinois broke thru the overburden of the Beacoup Mine. The mine was flooded so quickly that some miners were trapped inside. In 1918, the mine was finally pumped out and the body of a coal miner was found face down on the muddy floor of the mine. The mineral water of the creek had completely petrified his body. The preservation was so perfect that even his pipe and tobacco were intact.

Pope County

Satan's Ghost

Satan is buried in a private cemetery near Herod, Illinois. The Evil One is not the actual corpse buried in this haunted cemetery. This burial is that of Satan Parton. Unlike the Satan of the Bible, Satan Parton was an upstanding, respected and likeable person. The ghost of Satan loves to pull pranks on visitors to the cemetery. He is in the habit of hopping into cars parked nearby, putting them in gear and driving off a short distance.

The Golconda Madstone

In the early 1800s, Golconda was a wilderness area infected with snakes and various animals. As the settlers encroached on the natural habitat of the wildlife, some of the animals fought back by biting the unwary. Animal bites brought forth the fear of rabies. In pioneer times there was no cure for rabies, except for madstones.

The magical madstones could be found in the heads of toads and fish and could even be a hard object found in the stomach of a white deer. Some stones were discovered in creek beds or mines. These stones had the mysterious ability to drawl out toxins from the human body.

Madstones were considered extremely valuable. There were at least three known madstones in southern Illinois with the most famous being in Golconda. According to John W. Allen, the Golconda madstone was discovered in a coal mine and brought to Illinois from

Tennessee about 1870 by Matthew Trovillion. This madstone was so valuable that it was the subject of a lawsuit in 1911.

The proper way to use a madstone was to let it adhere to the area of the bite. After about an hour the madstone would fall off the wound. The stone would be placed in water until its surface would start to bubble. The process would be repeated until the stone would not adhere to the wound anymore. As if by miracle, the patient was cured.

The Golconda madstone was used hundreds of times on all kinds of bites with only one death due to the vicious wounds not rabies. No one knows for sure how the madstones worked and their whereabouts are a mystery today.

Pulaski County

Murder in Mound City, Illinois—the Murderer Hung

An 1884 Cairo correspondent of the St. Louis Democrat says:

On Saturday night last a desperado of considerable notoriety in that locality, named James Vaughn, in company with one of the operatives at Goodloe's foundry, name unknown, got on a spree and became inebriated to a considerable extent. Subsequently the two fell in with a carpenter or machinist from Pennsylvania, by name, John K. Charles, similarly inflicted. They continued together, and in the course of the evening's conversation, there seems to have been a clash of opinion between Vaughn's companion and Charles, resulting in a clash of arms, boots and fists. They closed, and in the ensuing struggle, Charles, proving to be the more sober man, got rather the better of the foundryman, observing which, Vaughn, who stood by, drew his pistol and deliberately shot Charles through the heart, killing him instantly.

Vaughn instantly disappeared, and crossing to Kentucky, fled. He was pursued however, Saturday, by Captain Ferrel and others, who overtook him about ten miles below Cairo. He was armed with a gun, which he presented, but was, nevertheless, captured without difficulty, taken back to Mound City, and lodged in jail, to await examination. A crowd gathered, went to the jail, armed with a log as a battering ram, affected an entrance, and taking Vaughn out, notified him that fifteen minutes would be generously allowed him to say his prayers and attend to any other matters he chose, preparatory to having his "mortal coil shuffled off." Hardly appreciating the reality of the thing at first, his cries when the truth began to break upon him are represented as heart-rendering--increasing in force and piteousness as the stolid indifference of his captors show how fixed was their purpose for blood, and how surely the retribution for his villainy was at hand.

Neither prayers nor cries could defer the appointed time, however, and at the minute he was run up a tree by the excited throng, where he hung till he was dead. He was left hanging till morning, when he was cut down by some of his friends and taken away. The thing was done determinedly, and at the scene of blood there seems to have been general unanimity of feeling. The appearance of his father, an individual enjoying considerable notoriety in the same way as his son, and his companion of Saturday night, had well-nigh cost them their lives, and they made themselves scarce suddenly.

Randolph County

Burned at the Stake for Witchcraft

Manuel, a slave, was burned at the stake for Witchcraft on June 15, 1779 in present day Randolph County, Illinois. The warrant for execution read as follows:

Illinois to Wit; To Richard Winston, esq., Sheriff in Chief of the District of Kaskaskia. Negro Manuel, a Slave, in your Custody, is condemned by the Court of Kaskaskia, after having made honorable Fine at the Door of the Church, to be chained to a post at the water side & there to be burnt alive, & his ashes scattered, as appears to me by Record. This Sentence you are hereby required to put in Execution on tuesday next, at 9 o'Clock in the morning; and this shall be your Warrant. Given under my hand & seal at Kaskaskia, the 13th day of June,- in the third year of the Commonwealth. I am, sir, yr hble servant, Jno. Todd

(NOTE - at the time, Illinois Territory was part of the Commonwealth of Virginia) No record of the actual execution has ever been found.

The Creole House

The Creole House is located in Prairie Du Rocher. It was built around 1800 by Dr. Robert McDonald. Two of the families who owned the Creole House lived in a 3 story mansion that stood just to the north of the house. This mansion mysteriously burned in 1867. The mansion was rebuilt and once again mysteriously burned just over a hundred years later in 1970.

No paranormal activity was reported until "haunted house" tours were started in 2005. "Ghost Effects" were set up in the Brickey Family cemetery behind the house. It almost seemed like someone or something was not very accepting of the activity. All of the electric equipment "fried." One evening, one of the haunted house actors looked in the bedroom window from outside and saw an old woman staring back at him. No one was in the house at the time. On the first night of the haunted house tour, all of the electricity shut down. An electrician was called to fix the problem. At that very moment, all of the electricity came back on. The circuit breakers were checked and none were found to have been tripped.

One of the rooms contains an old clock with a swinging pendulum that sits on the mantel. The clock was in perfect working order until the night of the haunted house tour, when it stopped on the stroke of 11:00. The clock has not worked since. When you are in the house and someone else enters, there is a very distinct, but difficult to describe sound no matter where you enter from. This sound can be heard, even when no one has entered.

Cold spots have been felt on many occasions. One caretaker came to the house one evening with four other people to take photographs of a mysterious image that appeared on the kitchen wall. The image is a bright light reflection through a window. The strange thing is that the entire window does not glare. Only the letters "I M" followed by a perfectly shaped skull. This appears to be an imperfection in the glass. All attempts to photograph the image have failed. All types of cameras have been tried including manual and auto focus cameras, digital and film cameras, cell phone cameras, flash and non-flash. No matter what is tried, the image cannot be captured with a camera. As the caretaker and guests were looking at the wall, a nearby chair began to move. It made an impression on the seat cushion as if someone was sitting on it. There was an extremely cold area of air above the seat.

There is only one room to enter the house from the outside and a key has to be used to open the door. When the door is unlocked it easily swings open with a nudge. One evening, the caretaker came back with some guests and as the door nudged open, it slammed shut with force! The caretaker tried to reopen the door, but it would not move. It was discovered that a folding chair was lying behind the door as if thrown there. No folding chairs are kept in that particular room and no one had been in the house. The door slamming incident has happened on more than one occasion.

One evening, one of the volunteers went out back to unplug some electric cords. There were lots of dried leaves covering the ground the volunteer heard very heavy, deliberate footsteps coming from around the corner. When he went to look for them, he discovered that no one was there. Random lights have been reported in the house by locals. The caretaker receives many calls from locals telling him that the lights are on and seem to come on "magically."

Many years ago, a local person committed suicide near the Creole House. He has been seen to the rear of the house. One night, two of the volunteers joked about the suicide, saying, "that's all I need is him running around the backyard!" At that very moment some of the black lights they had set up for the haunted house, started to flicker. The volunteer said, "Ya know, the spooks are gonna have it all turned off by starting time tomorrow!" Right then, the light went out leaving the volunteers in total darkness.

A volunteer was cleaning the house one day and felt a very cold spot in the bed room. Thinking a door was open, she checked the other rooms in the house and found them to be quite warm and all the doors barred. When she returned to the bedroom, it was warm just like the rest of the house.

One room contains photos of a family from the 1830s. These photos are generally crooked when you enter the house while all the other photos and paintings are always straight. One evening while straightening a rug in front of the corner cabinet (belonging to the first Governor of Illinois), the latches on the cabinet clicked and the glass doors slowly swung open. Later a light suddenly came on in the basement. This light could be seen through the knot holes in the parlor's wood floor. The strange thing was that the only access to the cellar was boarded shut several weeks previously.

One evening, as one of the volunteers was attempting to leave, he tripped and his car keys went flying. He heard them hit the metal of his car. He proceeded to feel around on the ground in the grass for about 15 or 20 minutes. When he got up, he discovered the keys were mysteriously hanging in the door lock.

The Little Egypt Ghost Society team of investigators encountered some unexplained paranormal activity while conducting a ghost hunt at this location. A moving ghost light orb was seen in real time, zipping from the parlor and into the kitchen area right behind me (witnessed by four people). There was the sound of footsteps running across the front porch. Several team members immediately went outside and could find no one near the house and no foot prints in the snow around the house. We recorded several unexplainable EMF readings using the Mel Meters, K2 meter, Ghost Meter and Cell Sensor meter. The PX device responded intelligently to questions asked.

Saline County

Pauper House Cemetery

The Saline County Pauper (or Poor) House is listed on the National Register of Historic Places. As early as 1819, the Illinois General Assembly enacted a "Pauper Bill" which required County Commissioners to appoint overseers of the poor. In an effort to care for the area's poor, land was purchased in 1863 and construction began in 1877 starting with a two-story Victorian style home that is now fitted with a museum of local and donated artifacts from the 1800s. Several log homes, a barn and blockhouse, an old Quaker church, jail house and a school completed the village.

Volunteers and visitors to the house have reported strange lights, voices, footsteps, cold spots and a chair that seems to rock on its own. Most anyone who has witnessed the activity of the home refuses to be left alone in the home or stay in it overnight.

The Pauper Cemetery contains some 263 crude stone markers with an estimated 60 belonging to children, dating back as far as 1849. Records indicate that not only people from the poor farm were buried here but that it was also the county burial site for unknown vagrants, rail road and coal mine victims, or abandoned children. The custom of the time was for those not having a proper funeral to be buried the same day as they were discovered dead, which did not leave a lot of preparation time for headstones resulting in some rather crude burial notes to be carved on the markers.

Some of these notes include; "Run over by a train at Wasson," "Gunshot wound," "Unknown baby found in sewer," "Gunshot wound administered by chief of Police," "Daddy," "Lithuania-wife still in Europe," "Found dead in ditch," "Carnival worker," "Murdered," "Left of Charlie Yates-O-Gara," "#3 mined accident," and "Shot by Charlie Birger at Ledford." Despite the large number of graves that have already been located the Historical Society is still searching for, and finding more unmarked graves.

Tuttle Bottoms Monster

Southern Illinois has long been known for its reports of monsters and strange happenings, and Tuttle Bottoms is no exception. The Tuttle Bottoms Monster was first reported in the 1960s in Tuttle Bottoms near Harrisburg, Illinois. On the north outskirts of Harrisburg is a section of town referred to as Dorris Heights. The middle fork of the Saline River passes through the woods of this scenic area. Hunters and people who would park along the road in that area would make frantic calls to police and sheriff departments reporting a large furry animal that resembled an overgrown anteater. Others said the creature resembled a large bear.

Strange tracks were often found nearby. In the 1960s and 70s, many high school kids would go to Tuttle Bottoms to drink beer and "make out." It was rumored that some murders took place in the Bottoms. Parents warned kids to stay away from that area. I remember one hot summer night in the late 1960s when our sitter took me and my brother for a ride through Tuttle Bottoms. As we crossed the bridge over the middle fork of the Saline

River, a large creature that resembled a prehistoric pterodactyl swooped down at the roof of the car, circled around and followed us for a short distance. Our sitter floored the gas pedal in her old car and we flew down that dark gravel road as fast as it could go. It was quite some time until I was brave enough to go back to Tuttle Bottoms

Demonic Forces in Eldorado Home

Our paranormal investigation team received a request to help rid a house of demonic activities. Upon arrival, the young couple who lived there explained that some unseen force had been attacking their baby. The baby slept in a crib in the front bedroom where the parents also slept. The parents stated that "something" unseen appeared to choke the baby as she slept and would shake the crib at times. The house was old and somewhat rundown in appearance. The ceiling sagged and the paneling on the walls was warped. A curtain served as a door between the living room and kitchen. The back bedroom had a small closet with a trap door that led to the attic. The entire house had a very depressing and oppressive atmosphere about it.

We conducted an Electromagnetic Field (EMF) sweep of the living room and front bedroom with our "Ghost Meter" EMF detectors and discovered very high EMF in the area of the crib while the rest of the room had no EMF. We decided to move the crib to another part of the bedroom that had no EMF. We then rechecked the area where the crib had previously stood and discovered that there was no EMF in that area. We then checked the crib with the EMF meters and discovered that the EMF was coming from the crib itself. We thoroughly searched the crib but could find no visible source for the EMF. Wherever we moved the crib, the EMF followed it. We then turned off all electric power to the house at the main switch to eliminate any man made sources of EMF.

Armed with flashlights, we performed another EMF sweep of the crib and found that it was still enveloped in a strong EMF field. Lisa and I went to the living room to discuss what might be causing the EMF when we both saw a "dark shape" run behind the curtain separating the living room and kitchen. Lisa and I were the only people in the house at that time and the family did not have any pets. We both ran into the kitchen to find whatever had run past the doorway and discovered that the room was empty and the back door was locked from the inside. We went outside and asked the other team members if they had seen anyone or anything enter or exit the house and they all reported that Lisa and I were the only ones that they saw.

We went back in the house with our St Benedict's Crosses and Holy Water to bless the crib, the bedroom and the entire house. We recited the Exorcism Prayer from the St Benedict's Cross and applied Holy Water to the entire area. We then went outside and blessed the four corners of the house. After the ceremony we once again check the crib for EMF and discovered that it had vanished. The entire house was free of the EMF fields. The house seemed to take on a new, brighter, happier appearance. It has been eight months since the exorcism and the family says that there have been no further occurrences of demonic attacks or activity.

Harrisburg Cinema 4 Ghost Hunt, Harrisburg

THEATER ONE – The only report of anything odd from theater one is an employee states that he saw the silhouette of a person looking out of the porthole at him.

THEATER TWO – An employee was vacuuming near the door when he felt a sudden cold chill and saw a large shadow to his right. There was nothing to his right and when he looked back it was gone. He said it was the most defined shadow he had ever seen.

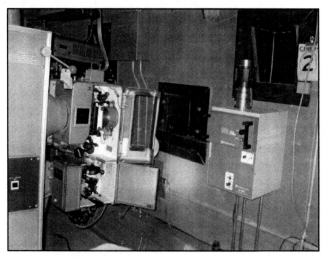

THEATER THREE – By far the most reports of paranormal activity have been in theater three and the hallway leading to it. Dan Beal, the manager of the theater, has heard several stories of employees seeing a dark figure of a man near the front rows of the auditorium from upstairs in the booth.. Customers have complained about someone moving the curtains when there was no one there. There is a wooden door at the end of the auditorium that leads to an area behind the screen. This door is known to open, close and even lock itself. Dan said that he has been in the building and noticed that the door will be in a different position than it was before. Dan has worked here longer than anyone and has never met an employee that has not felt "like someone was watching me" or "like someone else was there with me."

Last year he was sweeping the hallway leading to theater three and when he looked up from the floor onto the wall and the tall shadow man was on the wall right in front of me. Dan pretty much froze up and starred at it. Within seconds, he seemed to dematerialize like sand blows away in the wind. Everyone seemed to get a "bad" vibe from him. As Dan previously mentioned, there is a storage area behind the screen that leads into our warehouse. The employees say they feel like someone is in there watching them and they feel like whatever else is in there with them, seems to be behind the screen in the area. When employees have been in there alone, the area seems to have an odd "pull," like someone wants you to come back there. It is very hard to explain. Also, there is a small storage room near the entrance of the theater where we keep our posters. The light in there goes on and off by itself. The light is securely in place an there is no faulty wiring. There is one handicap seat in this auditorium that goes down by itself.

THEATER FOUR – Several employees swear that when they were in that theater they saw someone looking at them from the porthole in the booth. The theater is also known to have the areas where "cold spots" are felt.

LOBBY ONE and LOBBY TWO – Lobby one and two are hard to explain. While Dan has never heard anyone say anything about seeing something in either of the lobbies, it seems like when you are in one of them, you will hear something in the other and when you go to investigate, you just hear something in the other lobby. One thing that comes to mind is that the chandeliers have been reported to swing by themselves very slowly. On one occasion, a theater patron said he was watching them one day and a light started to turn on and then go off. He said he kept looking at it and when he looked at the light in the reflection of the front windows, there was the faint form of a small hand playing with the bulb.

RESTROOM 1 - Late one night, Dan was in the building alone standing in the concession area. He looked towards the ladies restroom near theater one and there was a little girl running out of it towards theater one. She was running the way a little kid would run to catch up with their parents. She had curly blonde hair and wore black shoes. She was faint, yet defined. One night while Dan was there with two friends conducting a ghost hunt, we heard knocking on the counter while we were in the restroom.

ARCADE – Dan has never heard of anyone seeing or feeling anything in the arcade. There are reports of employees hearing footsteps and muffled sounds of people talking in the office while the theater is closed.

BOOTHS – Booth one and two are in the same room. It is above the concession stand and it is where the projectors for theater one and two are located. It is a long room and the view is partially obstructed by the placement of the projectors. We have heard stories of people hearing things and sensing something coming from the far side of the booth.

Hungarian Cemetery

Hungarian Cemetery, also known as Hunky Dory Cemetery, is located near Ledford. This historic cemetery is rumored to be haunted. This secluded cemetery has been the scene of ghoulish activities such as grave robbing, grave desecration, satanic rituals, and animal slaughter and according to some rumors, human sacrifice. Blood and melted wax from black candles have been found on gravestones on many occasions.

If one is brave enough or foolish enough to enter the cemetery at night, they might be greeted by an elderly female apparition that walks the deserted road leading to it. Once seen, this phantom lady vanishes into the mist of the night. If you venture toward the far side of the cemetery, you may be able to see a glowing gravestone. Some say it glows all the time, others say it only reflects the moon light. This cemetery has a very sinister reputation and we do not recommend that you go there, even in daylight. It is known to be frequented by devil worshipers and meth users.

Salem Cemetery

Salem Cemetery located in Carrier Mills is, *or should I say was*, the location of a very mysterious grave. This above-ground burial contained the body of a young girl. On nights where there was a full moon the grave produced a vaporous mist that would creep along the ground. It seemed to be an intelligent mist in that it would inexplicably move toward and follow anyone nearby.

It was rumored that if you went to the grave at night and knocked on it three times and then go back to your car you would smell roses. This used to be a weekend ritual with many of the high school kids in the 1970s (myself included). One weekend night in the mid '70s, several of my friends and I decided to find out for ourselves. We drove out to the cemetery and located the grave near the back of the cemetery. I parked the car and we all got out and slowly crept over to the grave. After arranging ourselves in a circle around the grave, we all knocked three times, turned and ran towards our car. Looking behind us, we saw a wispy mist forming along the ground. The mist was slowly undulating along the ground towards us. At that moment we all smelled an overpowering scent of roses. We got out of there as fast as we could.

As if all of this was not mysterious and creepy enough, we decided to try to locate this grave again in 2008. The grave is not there anymore. What happened to it is a mystery. Was it relocated to discourage thrill seekers? No one seems to know, or if they do, they are not willing to say what happened to it.

Union County

The Lost Treasure of Union County

In the mid-1800s, an old man by the name of Miller would go to town to purchase various items and always paid for them with silver dollars. After many months, it was discovered that the silver dollars he used were counterfeit. The old man was arrested and put on trial for counterfeiting. During the trial it was decided to weigh the silver dollars. It was then discovered that the counterfeit silver dollars weighed more than the legal tender silver dollars and the judge decided to turn the man loose. While everyone was still in the court room, the old man paid his attorney with a fist full of silver dollars.

No one knew where the old man got the silver for the counterfeit dollars and he never told his secret to anyone. Some believed that it was Indian silver the old man had used. Legend says that an Indian chief once said that the white man had no judgment and if he had, he would shoe his horses with gold horse shoes. It was believed that a cave near Alto Pass, Illinois was full of gold. When the white man came to Union County, the Indians sealed the cave and no one has been able to find it since then.

Many years ago a man was digging a well near the site that the cave is believed to be located at. While digging, the man heard strange sounds coming from the hole. The deeper he dug, the louder the sounds became. Some people thought that the wind was causing the moaning sounds. Others said that the area was cursed and that the moans he heard were from long dead Indians.

Williamson County

Murder at Number Seven Row

In 1902, Number Seven Row was a town in Williamson County, Illinois. It was a coal mine town built by the Big Muddy Coal and Iron Company. Certain men in town were known for getting drunk and causing a big fuss. One night, three of the men got in a big fight. One of them was struck on the head with a hammer, killing him instantly. The other two men found a cheese knife nearby and hacked the dead man's head off with it. The dead man was carried a short distance away and thrown onto the middle of the Missouri Pacific Railroad tracks. His severed head was placed to the outside of the tracks.

The engineer of an oncoming steam locomotive pulling empty coal cars stopped the train just short of the dead man. No other trains had passed by since the day before and the body was still warm. The murderers were caught about an hour later. We have no idea what happened to the murderers. It is very likely that they were hung by an angry mob. Are these railroad tracks haunted today by the horror that took place there over 100 years ago? Go just east of Herrin, Illinois to the southwest quarter of the southeast quarter of Section 20 of Herrin Township and find out for yourself.

Witches of Williamson County

Milo Erwin, in the *History of Williamson County, Illinois* (1876), writes,

From 1818 to 1835, there were a great many witches in this county. The most noted one was an old lady by the name of Eva Locker, who lived on Davis' Prairie. She could do wonders, and inflict horrible spells on the young, such as fits, twitches, jerks and such like; and many an old lady took the rickets at the mere sound of her name. When she inflicted a dangerous spell, the parties had to send to Hamilton County for Charley Lee, the great witch-master to cure them. This he did by shooting her picture with a silver ball and some other foolery. It was a nice sight to see this old fool set up his board and then measure, point and cipher around like an artillery man planting his battery, while the whole family was standing around veiled and with the solemnity and anxiety of a funeral. None of the wizards of this county could do anything with Eva. They had to pale their intellectual fires and sink into insignificance before the great wizard of Hamilton County.

When a man concluded that his neighbor was killing too many deer around his field, he would spell his gun, which he did by going out early in the morning, and, on hearing the crack of his rifle he walked backward to a hickory wythe, which he tied in a knot in the name of the devil. This rendered the gun worthless until the knot was untied, or it might be taken off by putting nine new pins in the gun and fining it with a peculiar kind of lye, corking it up and setting it away for nine days. One old man told me he tried this, and it broke the spell. He had drawn right down on a deer just

111

before that, not over twenty steps distant, and never cut a hair. Cows, when bewitched, would go into mud holes and no man could drive them out; but the wizard, by laying the open Bible on their backs, could bring them out; or cut the curls out of their forehead and their tails off, and put nine pins in their tail and burn the curls with a poker. This would bring the witch to the spot, and then the matter was settled in the way our fathers settled their business.

Witches were said to milk the cows of the neighbors by means of a towel hung up over the door, when the milk was extracted from the fringe. If such deviltry was practiced now-a-days, the parties would be arrested for stealing. In place of having a herd of bobtailed cows, we have laws against cruelty to animals.

There was an idea that if you read certain books used by the Hard-shell Baptists, that the devil would appear. Happily for the honor of human nature, the belief in those foolish and absurd pretensions has been discontinued, for forty years by an enlightened public. Medical science has revealed remedies for those strange diseases whose symptoms were so little understood. The spell has been broken from the gun forever by untying the knot of ignorance, and letting the light of reason flood the mind.

George W. Sisney and the Bloody Vendetta

Those of you familiar with the "Bloody Vendetta" of the late 1800s in southern Illinois will be interested in my latest discovery. I have located the grave of one of the principal characters, Capt. George W. Sisney. He was a captain in the 81st Illinois Volunteer Infantry, Co. G during the Civil War and elected Sheriff in 1866.

The "Bloody Vendetta" started in 1862 with a disagreement between John Sisney and Marshall Crain. In 1869, there was a fight between Samuel Brethers, George W. Sisney and David Bulliner over a bunch of oats. In 1872 there was further trouble when Thomas Russell and John Bullinger started dating the same woman, Sarah Stocks. On Christmas Day in 1872, there was a riot in Carterville that involved the Sisneys and Crains.

On March 27, 1874, George and David Bullinger were killed in a shooting at church. On May 15, 1874, the Bullingers were involved in killing James Henderson. On July 28, 1875, George W. Sisney was shot and killed in his home by Marshall Crain.

George W. Sisney's home was located on the northeast corner of the square in Carbondale. The house extended eastward and faced south. On the night of July 28, 1875, George W. Sisney was sitting near a window on the south side of the house playing dominoes with one of his friends. An assassin was lurking on the porch in his sock feet and shot through the window. Sisney was struck by the shot under his left nipple leaving a hole about 2 inches in diameter. As he was shot, Sisney cried out "Oh, Lord, I am shot! Lord, have mercy on me!" Sisney remained seated upright in his chair for one and a half hours after he was shot dead. He was buried with full Masonic honors.

My wife and I located Capt. George W. Sisney's grave in a small unnamed cemetery on the south side of Old Route 13 about .2 miles from Division Street in the Crab Orchard Refuge. While walking through the cemetery just south of Sisney's grave, we both smelled the strong scent of lilacs and hyacinths. We looked everywhere, but could not find any flowers in the entire graveyard. The cemetery is very quiet and peaceful. We will be returning soon to conduct some EVP experiments and to take EMF and other readings. George W. Sisney was a captain in the Civil War and a Mason; perhaps I can give his spirit a direct order to respond to our experiments since I am a lieutenant colonel in the Army Reserve and a 32nd degree Mason?

The Grave of S. Glenn Young in Herrin City Cemetery

In the 1920s, the Ku Klux Klan in Williamson County was essentially a prohibition party. Prohibition law enforcement was the fundamental issue; race and religion had little to do with it. In 1923, the Klan began organizing in Williamson County, holding meetings attended by more than 5,000 citizens. The Klan in Williamson County drew large community support.

The Klan found a charismatic leader; S. Glenn Young, a former federal law enforcement officer. Federal authorities deputized the Klan to help enforce prohibition laws. Many public officials of Williamson County were allied with the bootleggers and were driven from office. They were replaced by Klan members. On Jan 24, 1925, Williamson County deputy sheriff (and bootlegger) Ora Thomas and S. Glenn Young shot and killed each other in a cigar store in downtown Herrin, Illinois.

The coroner's report of O.A. Jenkins, Undertaker, stated that one bullet entered the right breast of S. Glenn Young about two and a half or three inches below armpit. It ranged down and logged under the skin on left side four inches below left lower shoulder blade. Jenkins stated that he cut that bullet out. It was a .45 cal steel jacket bullet. The second bullet entered two and a half inches below the other bullet. It took a straight course coming out the left side. Both bullets went thru the heart. The bullet wounds were sufficient to kill. There was another wound on the little finger of the right hand that a bullet had grazed. It was about one inch long.

S. Glenn Young was buried in in full Klan regalia in this concrete vault built by William Lough and Sons. The casket was covered with between 18 to 20 inches of concrete and steel reinforcing on the top, bottom and sides.

The funeral of S. Glenn Young was attended by over 15,000 people.

Judge W.O. Potter Murders - 807 N. Market St. Marion

The bodies of the family members were found at the Potters residence at 807 N Market St. Marion by Judge Potter's surviving son Maurice as he returned home from a business trip around the time of 2:00 AM on the date of October 24th, 1926. All members of the family were dressed in night clothes and were all believed to have been killed sometime around 1:00 AM, the weapon is believed to have been a 20lb furnace shaker which was secured from within the basement of the house itself. Judge Potter himself was found in a cistern in the rear of the house where he had entered head first into 3 feet of water.

It is believed due to blood patterns and footprints found that Eloise (daughter) was killed first. The killer then surprised Lucille (daughter) in the bathroom and she was then killed by means of crushing her skull. Blood stains then lead across the hall to the room in which Lucille and the two young children were staying, Mrs. Potter is believed to have heard the children screaming, ran to help them and in doing so was also struck down by the killer. Eloise is thought to have not been killed immediately and was able to make her way to the bedroom where she died alongside her mother and the children. Bloody footprints were then followed down the back stairs.

In the hours before the murders there was nothing out of the ordinary about Judge Potter. His conduct was normal at the evening meal, and after dinner he read quietly while his granddaughters played around him. His son and daughter were dancing while a little granddaughter played a phonograph. As the surviving son was heading out for the night Judge Potter reportedly asked him to "come home early tonight." To those close to Judge Potter his deep depression was no secret, two of his brothers in law reported that he had relayed his despair unto them on the very morning that the family was found dead. Judge Potter had met Judge D.T. Hartwell in the lobby of the First National Bank and offered to help out, he spoke about how he had had a very bad night and that

117

he had been about to harm his little girl, "wouldn't that be awful" Potter had said of the incident, and mentioned that he did in fact feel better.

Conversations Potter had had with friends at the time led them to believe that he was going through great financial troubles. In his last weeks of life Judge Potter was known to have lost close to 30lbs and he would frequently break down crying. The controversy is that Judge Potter was convicted of the murder of his family members and of having taken his own life by means of drowning before the evidence in the case was even examined and the autopsy on Judge Potter revealed no water in the lungs and deep lacerations in his head.

Former residents of this house reported hearing sound of a struggle in the rear of the house as well as feeling unexplained cold spots in various rooms. Several years ago the house was torn down and all that remains is an empty lot, a depression in the yard where the cistern was and the grisly memories of murder.

Mysterious Happenings at Crab Orchard National Refuge Explosives/Munitions Manufacturing Area (EMMA) Operable Unit (OU)

Since the mid-1960s, there have been many reports of strange and unusual activity at the Crab Orchard Cemetery Area (COC) of the Crab Orchard National Refuge between Marion and Carbondale, Illinois. The Crab Orchard Cemetery Area is named due to the proximity of Hampton Cemetery which is located in an area of the Refuge that is closed to the public.

COC site #1 is approximately 100 x 200 feet. It contains a small circular depression near the center. An east/west oriented berm extends along the north end of the site. This site is suspected of formerly being a burial and detonation disposal area.

COC site #2 is approximately 250 x 350 feet and encompasses an old burn furnace and two depressions.

COC site #3 is a large area subdivided into two smaller areas. This site exhibits indications of explosives/munitions activity. A number of suspect berms and mounds with several detected magnetic anomalies are located within this site. The south side of this site is fenced and heavily wooded. Various sized pieces of TNT, metal debris and transite tile (contains asbestos) are scattered across the northern half of the site.

COC site #4 is located across the road and slightly north of COC site #3. It is rectangular and measures approximately 250 x 600 feet. This area is heavily wooded with a number of shallow depressions scattered throughout.

COC site #5 is a fenced, heavily vegetated area approximately 210 x 280 feet. A shallow depression is located in the southwestern corner of the site. TNT concentrations have been detected in the soil of this site.

COC site #6 is approximately 6 acres and is triangular in shape. This area is fenced and contains several depressions in the central and northern portions of the site. These depressions are the result of detonation disposal of TNT. There are many small metal fragments scattered around these depressions.

COC site #7 consists of approximately 2 acres of open area within a large field. An intact land mine was found at this site. The mine was destroyed by an exploded ordnance demolition (EOD) team.

COC site #8 is located in an open area within a field that is currently farmed. Magnetic anomalies have been found in this area.

COC site #9 is an irregularly shaped area approximately four acres in size. The area is heavily vegetated with fencing around the northern portion of the site. There are several man made depressions at this site. Two located near the southern end and the others located near the center and northern portions of the site.

COC site #10 is approximately 120 feet square and consists of a fenced area on the northern edge of a corn field. There are 85 bunkers in Area 13 that were built for the storage of 500-pound bombs. Many of the bunkers are currently used by Olin Corporation and U.S. Powder to store explosives.

Oliver, a former security guard for one of the government contractors in the ORDIL area, reported that on several occasions he observed and was stalked by what he described at a seven foot tall humanoid creature covered with light brown matted hair covered in mud. This creature closely matched the description of the Big Muddy Monster (actually a hoax – details on file with Little Egypt Ghost Society) that had been reported in the Murphysboro, Illinois area in the mid '70s.

Farmers and hunters in the area have reported sightings of a half man half bat-like creature with glowing red eyes. It has been seen flying out of a wooded area, landing near a pond where it appeared to take a drink and then would circle the field before returning to the wooded area.

Ghost lights have also been seen hovering and bouncing around the depressions found in the various COC areas of the refuge. They are described as orange in hue and vary in size from that of a baseball to larger than a beach ball.

There have been various reports of UFO activity over the refuge. A young couple was parked near one of the access roads and reported seeing a large triangular shaped object fly overhead in a northwest to southeast direction. It appeared just above treetop level and made no sound as it traveled at great speed. A man was riding his motorcycle in the refuge when he decided to pull to the side of the road to relieve himself in the ditch. He said as soon as he zipped up his pants, he was "buzzed by three glowing balls of light." They emitted a humming and sound and he felt like he was vibrating as if he was having an MRI exam. These stories are only the tip of the iceberg when it comes to high strangeness at the Crab Orchard Wildlife Refuge. Since most of the area is closed to the public, we will probably never know what lurks within its boundaries.

Creepy New Developments at the Old Crab Orchard Munitions Area

Story by Lisa Cline.

Bruce asked me to go photograph different areas for our book. So my son Christopher and I decided late one afternoon to go to the old munitions area and have a look around. We drove out to the Crab Orchard Munitions Area and when we arrived there the air seemed to have a really tense feeling to it. The air was stifling and made us feel restless.

We decided to get out of the car and start taking photos regardless of how tense we were feeling. I began taking photos of the area and noticed that there was a dark hand-like object on the images. Thinking I must have somehow got my hand in the way, I retook the photos and noticed that the dark object was still in some of the images. Then, my camera stopped working even though it had fresh batteries and a new memory card in it. No matter what I tried, my camera would not work.

I got out my other camera and started taking photos of the old munitions bunkers and noticed that the same dark hand like object was on these images as well. As I continued to photograph the area, the second camera

I was using malfunctioned and would not turn on again. Finally, after resting with it for a few minutes, I was able to resume photographing the area, but noticed that some images would not turn out.

As I was photographing, my son said, "Mom, did you hear that?" and we both looked at one another and thought someone was near us shooting an old gun. We heard a sound like, "Pow, pow, pow, pow" and for a few seconds there was quietness. Then we heard it again, "Pow, pow, pow, pow." We decided we had better get back in the car. Knowing the area had armed guards, we decided maybe we should leave.

The air began to feel even tenser. As we got back into the car, my son looks in the mirror and said, "Um, mom, look." As I looked up, I saw a black shadow object that looked like a WWII soldier behind our car. I asked my son what he saw and he said, "Mom, it was a soldier bent down like he was about to fight." As we left we were discussing the things that had happened. We check the cameras and noticed that they were once more in perfect working order.

Crab Orchard Lake

In 1936, work was started on the Crab Orchard Creek Project. The purpose of this project was to construct three lakes for recreational use and as an industrial water supply. To make way for the proposed lake, a portion of Illinois Route 13 between Marion and Carbondale had to be relocated about a half mile to the north. Crab Orchard Lake was completed in 1939 by the Works Progress Administration (WPA). There are portions of Old Route 13 that still lie beneath the waters of Crab Orchard Lake. During times of extreme drought, boaters can catch a glimpse of the old road. Several night-time boaters have reported sightings of ghostly lights under the water in the vicinity of where the old road lies. Could these lights that are seen be the phantom cars of the 1920s and '30s that used to travel the old route?

Violent History, Mystery and Hauntings Lie Buried in the Cemeteries of Marion

On October 24, 1926, Judge W. O. Potter and his family were found dead at their family home located at 807 N. Market Street (now a vacant lot). At the time, it was thought that Judge W. O. Potter murdered his wife, two daughters and two granddaughters and that afterwards he committed suicide by jumping down a well in the back yard. My research has led me to believe that the Potter family murders were committed by the Williamson County Knights of the Ku Klux Klan. The Potter family is buried on the west side of the Goddard Chapel in Old Rose Hill, Block 13, Lot 40.

Another brutal murder was that of an Illinois State Trooper of dubious repute, Lory Price, his wife Ethel, and their unborn child. Trooper Price was tied in with certain Williamson County car thieves. The thieves would steal cars and then tell Price where to recover them. The thieves and Trooper Price would then split the reward money. At some point, Price and Charlie Birger had a falling out. On January 17, 1927, Price and his wife were abducted from their home and taken away in separate cars by gangsters. Price's body was found 2 days later riddled by 18 gunshot wounds. His wife's body was found at the bottom of a mine shaft 4 months later. Trooper Price and his wife are buried in Odd Fellows Cemetery, Block A, Lot 1.

Rado Millich was the last man to be hanged in Williamson County. Millich was a member of the Charlie Birger gang. He was tried and convicted of murder. On January 21, 1927 he was taken from his cell in the Williamson County Jail and hanged in the alley (now known as Paradise Alley). He is buried in the potter's field at Rose Hill Cemetery.

Ma Hatchett

During the 1920s, Colp, Illinois was a rip snortin', wide open town with a wild reputation. The town boasted several coal mines nearby and even more taverns. Such was the renown of Colp that Ike and Tina Turner once

125

performed there. The entertainment offered in Colp was second to none, and the most sought after entertainment was offered at a place known as Ma Hatchet's. She purchased the tavern, restaurant, brothel in 1923. It consisted of her house with a six bedroom addition attached by passageways. Men would come from all the surrounding communities to partake of some very special entertainment that Ma Hatchet offered. You see, Ma Hatchet's place was a brothel.

Ma Hatchet would only hire black girls and would only let them service white men. If any of her girls were caught with a black man, they would be sent packing. All the women were clean, well dressed and poised. They all had regular checkups with a local doctor. The going rate for Ma Hatchet's ladies was $5 to $50 depending on their specialty. One man sent a letter to a local newspaper stating that he had been to Ma Hatchett's place many times and considered it to be the best and cleanest brothel in 37 states and five foreign countries. He went on to say that he had personally seen several respected members of the community there such as doctors, ministers, lawyers, and business men.

Ma Hatchett became very wealthy with her business venture. She was very civic minded and gave freely to local charities and those in need. In 1957, the Illinois State Police raided Ma Hatchett's, shutting it down after more than 30 years of service to the public. Even after Ma Hatchett's was shut down, many of her girls continued their profession with their favorite customers.

A Pioneer Cemetery

A lonely cemetery is located in Williamson County on Rocky Comfort Road between Little Grassy Lake and Devil's Kitchen Lake. During the early 1800s, a pioneer family was traveling west through southern Illinois to what they hoped would be their new homestead. At some point during their journey, the entire family contracted the highly contagious disease of the "Pox."

The settlers of the Lick Creek were very concerned about the possibility of being infected with the pox from these strangers. They quickly decided that the only safe thing for them to do was to corral the infected pioneers in a certain area and to place guards nearby so that they would not escape and possibly infect others. The orders given to the guards were "shoot to kill" if any tried to leave the quarantine area.

This vigil was kept over the pioneers until every one of them had died. It was decided to wait until the bodies had been picked clean by scavengers before burial. Only when the bodies were picked clean down to the bone, were the unfortunates buried.

Jailhouse Ghost

County jails are known for intrigue, tragedy, and terror. Going to jail can be a scary experience, especially if your bunkmate is a dead man.

In the spring of 1986, Calvin was arrested for conspiracy to commit murder. He allegedly offered an undercover law enforcement officer $500 to kill his wife. This act landed Calvin in the Williamson County Jail in Marion, Illinois. He was assigned to one of the top bunks in "E" Block. During the early morning hours of the midnight shift, the correctional officers were alerted to yells and screams coming from the inmates of "E" Block. One of the inmates who shared a cell with Calvin was hysterical. He had awakened from a fitful sleep by a warm, sticky, wet dripping sensation from the bunk above his. There was a towel draped over the side of the bunk that appeared to be wet and dark. On closer observation it was evident that it was fresh BLOOD... and lots of it too.

Calvin had taken his eye glasses and broken the lenses out of them. He used the broken lenses to slash the veins and arteries inside both elbows. He bled to death in about 20 minutes. Correctional staff and ambulance personnel removed Calvin's body from the cell and the inmates were given mops and buckets to clean up the bloody mess.

Former correctional officers reported that a few nights later strange things began to happen in the jail on the midnight shift. The electronic doors in the cellblocks that were operated by an officer in Central Control would mysteriously open and close all by themselves. Security gates in one of the hallways would malfunction and open and close also. Many of the superstitious inmates were of the opinion that the ghost of Calvin was causing the electrical disturbances. No logical explanation for the doors and gates opening and closing was ever found.

White County

The Man Whose Hobby Was Being a Hangman

George Phillip Hanna was a southern Illinois banker, farmer and volunteer hangman. He was born in Epworth, White County, Illinois on September 16, 1873 and became one of the wealthiest landowners in White County, Illinois. He witnessed his first hanging at age 22 in McCleansburg, Illinois in 1896. When the prison crew bungled the job, Hanna said that it was "brutal, horrifying." Hanna decided to get his own rope and study hanging. The rope he used for hanging was handmade 4-ply long fiber hemp that he purchased for $65 in St Louis, Missouri.

Although Hanna officiated at 70 hangings, he stated, "I haven't much nerve" and "I dread hangings. I'm upset for days before and afterwards. When I hanged Birger, a bad man, I hid the noose behind my back until the cap was adjusted." Hanna thought that he could perform hangings better if he used his own equipment. He built a portable scaffold that stood over 15 feet tall. This scaffold was used for the first time in Murphysboro, Illinois for the hanging of a black man. The hoods used to cover the head of the person to be hung were sewn by Hanna's wife. The prisoner was given their choice colors, black or white. Hanna would visit each prisoner before the execution and tell them "I am here to help you." He told them that he would try to spare them any misery and assured them that their death would be painless.

Most of the hangings went according to plan, some did not and some were even brutal. During one hanging in 1920, the condemned man fell to the ground and was severely injured when the rope broke. Hanna ran down the steps of the scaffold, picked up the condemned man and carried him to the floor of the scaffold. The man shouted out, "Hurry up, boys, and get me out of my misery."

After each execution, Hanna would refuse payment but would make one simple request…that he be given the weapon used to the commit the crime. Among the weapons once used by men he executed is the machine gun used by Charlie Birger in the Birger-Shelton gang feud, an axe, a rag-wrapped brick, a shotgun and numerous other murderous items. Hanna died September 6, 1948 in Evansville, Indiana.

Note: Charlie Birger was offered the customary choice of either a white or black hood by hangman Hanna. Birger's reply was "I'm not a kluker" (referring to the Ku Klux Klan that was fighting bootleggers in southern Illinois during the 1920's). Birger was hung wearing a black hood.

Bibliography

Allen, John W. *It Happened in Southern Illinois.* Carbondale: Southern Illinois University Press. 1968.

Allen, John W. *Legends and Lore of Southern Illinois.* Carboondale: Southern Illinois University Press. 1963.

Callary, Edward. *Place Names of Illinois.* University of Illinois Press. 2009.

Erwin, Milo. *The History of Williamson County Illinois.* Williamson County Historical Society. 1876.

The Historic Town Square Carbondale, Illinois. City of Carbondale Development Services Department. 1997

Hale, Stan J. *Williamson County Illinois Sesquicentenniel History.* Turner Publishing. 1993.

Iseminger, William R. *Cahokia Mounds: America's First City.* The History Press. 2010.

Jung, Jim. *Weird Egypt.* Wooley Worm Press. 2006.

Lansden, John M. *A History of the City of Cairo Illinois.* Southern Illinois University Press. 1910.

Magee, Judy. *Cavern of Crime.* Riverfolk Publishing Co. 1973.

Moore, Mary Jo. *The Potter Family Tragedy.* Marion Living Magazine. May 2007.

Paisley, Oldham. *Oldham Paisley's Scrapbooks.* Williiamson County Historical Society.

The History of Saline County. Saline County Genealogical Society. 1997.

Legacies of Little Egypt. Southern Illinoisian. D-Books Publishing, Inc. 1997.

About the Authors

Bruce Cline is a paranormal investigator and ghost historian. He was born and raised in Southern Illinois and currently lives in Carbondale, Illinois with his wife Lisa. He received B.S. and B.A. Degrees from Southern Illinois University in Carbondale, Illinois.

Bruce is a former law enforcement officer and currently works as a Radiologic Technologist specializing in CT/MRI and is a Corps of Engineers Lieutenant Colonel in the Army Reserve. He is also an Illinois licensed Funeral Director and Embalmer.

Bruce has had a long time fascination with history, folklore and ghost stories. While in high school, he started the GASLIGHT GHOST CLUB which would meet in his backyard tree house to tell ghost stories.

In 2007 the LITTLE EGYPT GHOST SOCIETY was formed by Bruce and Lisa Cline. Since that time, Bruce and Lisa have traveled extensively throughout the Midwest in search of the history, mystery and hauntings of interesting people, places and things.

The LITTLE EGYPT GHOST SOCIETY has been featured in the Southern Illinoisan, Harrisburg Daily Register and the Daily Egyptian newspapers. They have also been featured on WRUL and WROY radio as well as WSIU-TV.

Little Egypt Ghost Society

Southern Illinois

The LITTLE EGYPT GHOST SOCIETY is a non-profit research group based in Carbondale, IL. We are dedicated to assisting those who may be experiencing paranormal activity. Our goal is to explore the history, mystery and hauntings of Southern Illinois and ultimately strive for clearer knowledge of the supernatural.

Our approach to investigating paranormal activity is scientific. We attempt to document claims of paranormal activity using a variety of state of the art, multi-media equipment. All findings are carefully reviewed by our team of paranormal experts with an open yet skeptical mind to rule out any possible natural causes.

The LITTLE EGYPT GHOST SOCIETY does not claim to have all the answers but our experience and knowledge of the field has allowed us to provide accurate results.

CPSIA information can be obtained at www.ICGtesting.com
Printed in the USA
242439LV00001B/26/P

9 780979 040115